The Gunner's Guide to Law School

THE Gunner's Guide TO Law School

Marc A. Silverman

Carolina Academic Press
Durham, North Carolina

Library of Congress Cataloging-in-Publication Data

Names: Silverman, Marc A., author.
Title: The Gunner's guide to law school / by Marc A. Silverman.
Description: Durham, North Carolina : Carolina Academic Press, LLC, [2020]
Identifiers: LCCN 2020032519 (print) | LCCN 2020032520 (ebook) | ISBN 9781531020354 (paperback) | ISBN 9781531020361 (ebook)
Subjects: LCSH: Law schools--United States. | Law--Study and teaching--United States.
Classification: LCC KF272 .S565 2020 (print) | LCC KF272 (ebook) | DDC 340.071/173--dc23
LC record available at https://lccn.loc.gov/2020032519
LC ebook record available at https://lccn.loc.gov/2020032520

Carolina Academic Press
700 Kent Street
Durham, North Carolina 27701
Telephone (919) 489-7486
Fax (919) 493-5668
www.cap-press.com

Printed in the United States of America

To NCC for believing in me and helping me get into law school
To my mother for her never-ending support
To my wife for carrying me through
To my daughters for their future

Contents

Introduction

I'm not the smartest guy in the room. I don't work harder than other people. My standardized test scores were mediocre. I got rejected from nearly every law school. Yet once I got in, I got nearly straight As. And I graduated first in my class. The reasons are in this book. Success in law school does not require innate ability; it does not require genius; it is purely mechanical. No more than simple logic, preparation, and dedication. If you can understand the basic frameworks and apply them consistently, then you will succeed in law school. And you may even be in the top 10% of your class.

This book provides those frameworks. Frameworks are important in the law. Every law is simply a framework of rules that you plug facts into. It is entirely a matter of basic logic. If you know how to set up the problem, then you can get the right answer for any problem. And the good thing about law school is that there are no *right* answers; if you can spot the issue, identify the rules, and plug in the facts, then that is all you need. You can spin the facts however you want so long as you do so within the right framework. You will stay ahead of the curve if you can spot the issue, apply the rule, and reason correctly. That's it. And you will be able to do that no matter the course if you follow the basic frameworks in this book.

This book starts with a chapter on how to think. And by that I do not mean "thinking like a lawyer." In fact, you should not be thinking like a *lawyer* in law school; you should be thinking like a *law student.* A law student has one goal—to be a lawyer. To be the lawyer you want to be you must be successful in law school. And success in law school is measured by one thing: grades. Whatever type of lawyer you want to be, law school is simply too expensive, too time consuming, and too stressful for you to be anything but fully invested.

Surprisingly though, law school is not full of driven, hard-working, or even smart people—it is full of people who just want to get by, get their degree, and rake in the cash. They are less interested in *learning* the law than being *told* the law. They come to class expecting a handout with the black letter law. But that is not how law school works. Law school teaches you a process; not the answers. That is because practicing law is about the process—not the answers. When a client comes to a lawyer with a problem, the lawyer doesn't know the answer. A good lawyer doesn't pretend to. What a good lawyer knows is where to find the rules and how to apply the rules. Law school teaches you those skills. Students who expect the law handed to them miss that fundamental point. That is why this book encourages you to embrace the process. Be a gunner.

If you haven't heard the term "gunner" yet, it is generally an insult in law school. Urban dictionary defines it as:

> A person (usually a medical or law school student) who uses over 3 different colored highlighters, tabs every page in their notebook, and raises their hand after every question asked by their professor, regardless of if they know the correct answer or not. Gunners like to hear themselves speak. They use complicated words to make themselves sound smart even though they have no idea what's going on in class—they pretend they do. They are trying to intimidate you and eliminate competition.[1]

There are certainly some aspects of that definition you want to avoid. You don't want to be someone who raises their hand for every question for the sake of hearing their own voice. You don't want to be someone who uses big words to sound smart. And you don't want to be someone focused on competition. But you *do* want to be fully invested. And a gunner, if anything, is fully invested. If it takes you three-colored highlighters to brief a case, do it. If you want to tab out your notebook, so be it. And if you want to answer questions in class, you should do that. Indeed, throughout this book, you will find references to studies that show that the mere act of doing some of those things boosts your ability to learn. For example, writing in the text as you read helps you learn and remember better. Participating in class boosts your comprehension and allows you to test your learning in real time. Neuroscience confirms that these acts activate the brain in ways that cause you to become more invested, more attentive, learn more material easier, and even retain more information.

1. http://www.urbandictionary.com/define.php?term.

Another lesson neuroscience teaches us is that attitude affects performance. That is because your brain is a goal-striving machine. It works automatically toward goals and expectations about the world. Some goals and expectations, like survival, are automatic and subconscious. They work without your input. When you see a lion, you are hard-wired to expect it to kill you. Your adrenaline automatically pumps, and you run. But as a person with a conscious mind, you can choose goals and shape your expectations. Expect success and understanding and you will find it; expect difficulty and you will find that instead. The same with law school. Study after study confirms that your attitude influences your performance. If you think it will be easy, then your brain is primed to accept that. On the other hand, if you think it will be hard, then it will be. In other words, whether you think you can, or you think you can't, you are right. That is why chapter one discusses the mental framework you need for law school. Because without the right mental framework, you will fail.

Of course, thinking positively is not enough. That merely provides a foundation. From there, the most important framework is the logic of arguments. An argument is not two people yelling at each other. An argument is more like a mathematical proof. The basic form of argument in law school is called a syllogism. A syllogism is a three-step proof—it has a rule (a major premise), facts (the minor premise), and a conclusion. In law school, you are always given the rule and the facts, and all you must do is put it together. The only wrinkle about law school (and the law), is that there are syllogisms upon syllogisms. In other words, the rule statement typically needs to be unpacked into narrower syllogisms. For example, the rule statement for enforceability of a contract may be that it requires an offer, consideration, and acceptance. But to understand an "offer" or "consideration" or "acceptance," each one of those terms must be broken down into its own syllogism. And sometimes, the breakdown of the rule within the rule needs another syllogism. So what you get are syllogisms upon syllogisms. If you can understand that basic form, then you will succeed in any law school class and any exam, including the bar exam. Chapter one explains this form.

From there, you are ready to begin learning—that means class. In chapter two, we move to class frameworks. Many students blow off class or don't take it seriously. But remember that law school is about teaching you how to be a lawyer. And being a lawyer does not mean knowing all the answers; it means knowing how to spot the questions and then knowing how to find the answers. That means law professors do not just tell you the law. They use the Socratic method to pull it out of you. And the only way they can pull it out of you is if there is something there to pull out. That means you must know the material *before* you come to class. That means reading. Reading law, however, is not like other reading. Reading law is an active process. It requires you to *understand* the case. To understand a case, you need to develop active reading techniques that require participation with the text. One way you can do that is to read with a pen and write in the text. Circle, underline, and most importantly, summarize in the margins.

But class preparation doesn't end after reading the cases. The best students take class seriously. That means participation. In some cases, professors even give a half-grade bump to those students that participate. But even more important, participation keeps you engaged in class. It tests your knowledge. And it gives you an opportunity to test your skills on your feet. Doing so will help prepare you for the exam. After all, the exam itself is a stressful situation where unknown facts are thrown at you and you must respond within a short time. The more you test yourself to think on your feet in class, the better prepared you will be when you get to the actual test.

In chapter three, we look at exam frameworks. There are two important steps to preparing for the exam: creating an outline of the law you have learned throughout the semester, and taking practice tests. Creating an outline is hard and time-consuming. But doing it yourself is necessary. Outlining is more than just having the answers ready; it is about taking the time to grapple with the rules you've learned and organizing them in a way that makes sense to you. If you can distill and organize the rules, it means you really understand them. Students who use a commercial outline or one from another student miss that. The work you put into creating the outline is just as important as having the outline itself. If you do it right, you might even find that you don't need to reference it during the exam (most professors allow you to take a self-prepared outline into the exam). Moreover, by creating the outline yourself, as an added benefit, you will have created a mental map of your outline that will ease your cognitive strain during a test. Chapter three discusses how to create that outline.

Chapter three also discusses the next step in acing an exam, which is practice. An exam is more than a test of knowledge—it is a performance test. And while you can't anticipate the exact question you will get on an exam, you will be able to practice reading a prompt and writing down the rules that match. You should practice under the same time pressure and, if possible, by using your professor's old exams. If you take at least two practice tests, you will find that by the time you take the second one, you will be faster. You will be able to find the rules you need faster and write them out faster. As those tasks become automated, your mind will be free to focus on the application. By easing that burden, you are freeing up mental resources you will need during the exam. The more you practice, the more skilled you become at reading and analyzing an exam prompt, and the more skilled you are, the stronger your exam writing will be.

That brings us to taking the exam. Using the active-reading techniques discussed in chapter two will be key. Just as you did when studying for class, on exam day, you will engage with the text by circling, underling, and writing in the margin. That will help you identify the issues and important facts as you read. Writing in the margins will help create a mini-outline that you use to write the exam. Once you are ready to write the exam, you use a familiar format that all law students and professors will recognize—IRAC. IRAC stands for issue, rule, application, and conclusion. That form is important to use because it is the most simple and proper argument format discussed above, which is the syllogism. IRAC also satisfies your professor's expectations about what an exam should *look* like, which invokes the fluency-effect. That means that if you write the exam in a format they expect, it will be easier for your professor to read, which in turn means that they are more likely to judge that information favorably. More importantly, failing to follow that format invokes the opposite of the fluency-effect, which is that the information is harder to read and that causes your professors to form a negative assessment of your writing just by its form. So, do yourself a favor and follow IRAC. By actively reading your exam, you will have all the issues spotted in the margins. Then you use the outline you created in the margin to find the rule, write it down, and apply the facts to that rule.

In chapter four, we discuss frameworks for classes that require you to write papers rather than take exams. In your first year, you will undoubtedly take a class on legal writing where you will learn the basics of writing. You will produce several different kinds of legal writing, such as a memorandum and a brief. The first, second, and third rule for these classes is to follow your professor's rule. For example, your professor may give you rules as to font, format, type size, spacing, etc. Even in the real world, courts and judges have requirements as to format that you must follow. It is necessary that you follow those rules. The same is true in your paper courses. Once you have those rules down, you can move on to writing technique. The basic format for any legal writing is the same as the exam—IRAC. But there are differences within that structure, such as the way you draft an issue statement and the depth you discuss rules and cases. And the most important difference between exam writing and paper writing is creating an outline of what you are going to write before you actually start to write. Creating an outline before you write is a necessary step in writing an actual paper—skipping it is a false economy. Indeed, a proper outline will take away most of the pain of writing. If you draft a good outline, then the paper will write itself.

Beyond exams and paper classes are the many activities offered in law school. But there are only two that are important: law review and moot court. After securing your grades, making law review and moot court are the two most important markers for success in law school. That is why, in chapter five, we discuss how to make law review and moot court board—from the write-on to the oral argument.

In chapter six, this book will discuss considerations for choosing upper level courses, clinics, externships, and working while in law school. At bottom, each one is based on time management. As a lawyer, time is your commodity. You will schedule it, track it, and bill for it. As a law student, your schedule can make or break your ability to succeed. You can take all the interesting classes you want, overload yourself with clinics, and work two jobs, but you must protect your time so that you can put the required work into each class and graduate law school with the highest grades possible.

In chapter seven, this book will provide some tips for beyond law school—specifically, your first years as an associate in a law firm. Transitioning to practice from law school is not easy, but there are some basic tips that can help you succeed.

In the end, this book provides frameworks and guidelines for law school. You can apply them to any class you take in law school. No matter what the subject, the approach is always the same. Like practicing law, law school is all about a formula. And so is this book. A good formula for success provides not only the tools you need to succeed, but also provides confidence that allows you to handle the stress while focusing on the substance. None of this is to say that law school is easy. It is not. Law school takes dedication and many, many hours of work. But it is not beyond anyone's grasp. By using the techniques in this book, you will be confident that you know how to succeed in any law school class. You may even enjoy it.

The Gunner's Guide to Law School

CHAPTER ONE

Fundamental Frameworks

The substance of law school is not difficult. In fact, the law is (supposed to be) written so that everyone can understand and apply it. Juries of nonlawyers come together every day to apply and interpret the law to the facts presented to them. Sure, they misapply it sometimes, but the concepts are accessible to anyone. And I assure you, they are available to you as well. You do not need to be a genius to be a great lawyer, and you certainly do not need to be a genius to succeed in law school.

The reason why some people succeed and others fail has little to do with intelligence; just like anything else, success starts with how you think. While you can't simply will yourself to succeed, the way you think about law school influences your ability to learn. That is because your brain is a goal-striving machine. It works automatically toward goals and expectations about the world.

Some goals and expectations, like survival, are automatic and subconscious. They work without your input. When you see a lion, you are hard-wired to expect it to kill you, so your adrenaline automatically pumps and you run. But because you also have a conscious mind, you have the ability to choose goals and shape your expectations. Expect success and understanding and you will find it; expect difficulty and you might find that instead.

Study after study confirms that your attitude influences your performance. It has been demonstrated that your mind cannot distinguish between real memories and vividly imagined and repeated ones. That means that those who "practice" their skills through vivid imagination actually do better when using those skills. And the opposite can happen with negative practice; trick yourself into believing things are difficult or that you have certain negative traits and you will end up believing it and acting on it. In other words, as the old saying goes, "whether you think you can or whether you think you can't—you're right."[1] That is more than just a saying. Study after study has confirmed that our attitude influences our abilities.[2] That means that those who think they will succeed are far more likely to do so than those who think they won't.

I. Mental Framework

A. Your Attitude Influences Your Performance

The reason that your attitude influences your performance has to do with the connection between your conscious and unconscious mind. Your conscious mind is the part of your brain that you control, and the unconscious mind is the part you do not control. The conscious mind directs planning, thoughts, and actions to reach goals.[3] It is, at bottom, a goal-striving machine.[4] And because we are in control of our conscious mind, we get to pick some of our goals.

Other goals, however, like staying alive, are automated by our unconscious mind. Your unconscious mind automates tasks for survival goals because it could not function otherwise. Your unconscious mind constantly processes information from your senses, and in doing so, takes in a staggering eleven million bits of information every second. Without an unconscious mind to

---

1. This quote is typically attributed to Henry Ford, but many other historical figures have said similar statements, and the thought dates back to Virgil in the Aeneid, who wrote, *Possunt quia posse videntur*, "for they can conquer who believe they can." *See* https://quoteinvestigator.com/2015/02/03/you-can/.

2. *See generally*, Jennifer A. Mangels, et al., *Why do beliefs about intelligence influence learning success? A social cognitive neuroscience model* (2006) ("There is increasing evidence that the likelihood of their success is influenced not only by actual ability, but also by the beliefs and goals that they bring to the achievement situation.").

3. Leonard Mlodinow, *Subliminal: How Your Unconscious Mind Rules Your Behavior*, at 102 (2012).

4. For a long time, cognitive scientists have analogized the mind to a computer. The Computer Representational Understanding of Mind ("CRUM") assumes that "the mind has mental representations analogous to data structures and computational procedures similar to algorithms." Paul Thagard, *Mind: Introduction to Cognitive Science*, at 11 (2d ed.) (2005); Daniel Kahneman, *Thinking Fast and Slow*, at 71 (2011) ("We have in our head a remarkably powerful computer, not fast by conventional hardware standards, but able to represent the structure of our world by various types of associative links in a vast network of various types of ideas."). Indeed, cognitive psychology treats people "as information systems that process [] mental states much in the way a computer processes data." Mlodinow, at 97.

process all that information automatically and quickly, your mind "would freeze like an overtaxed computer."[5] That, of course, would be devastating for your basic survival. As a result, survival goals are automated by the unconscious mind to ensure survival.

But survival goals are not the only things the unconscious mind can automate—the unconscious mind can also automate complex behaviors, like sports, social interactions, learning, and reading, to name just a few. To automate behavior, the mind creates mental scripts to handle information, and those mental scripts, in turn, are based on our expectation of how the world works. This expectation function arises because your senses are not perfect; the raw data we get from our senses has gaps in it. For example, there are blind spots in your vision; there are sounds you do not hear; there are tastes you miss. Your mind has to fill in those gaps to make sense of the world, and it does so through expectation.

Take vision as an example. Our eyes have blind spots and each eye sees the world from different angles (try looking at something close up and alternating closing one eye; it's slightly different). But, in your everyday vision, you don't see blank spots and you don't see objects constantly shifting perspective. That is because our mind merges the images and fills in gaps based on expectations of the world.

Same thing with reading. It's why yuor barin can raed tihs without struggling. Your brain accomplishes these tasks unconsciously based on contextual clues. It does so to create models of the world for you to understand, and to understand it quickly. It is not about perfection; it is about survival.

Consider memory as another example. Our minds are not great at recording events. We simply receive too much information. So, instead, our memory retains a general gist of events; it does not retain all the details. As a result, when you are asked to recall those details, your unconscious mind actually fills in those gaps by making up details that are consistent with your expectations of what would have occurred. That is why eyewitness accounts are so often wrong or conflicting. People remember the important things from an incident—the crash, a person hurt, two cars—but they do not remember the details such as the person's face, the color of the car, or the time of day. That is because those details are not important to your survival. So if we are pressed to remember the details, then our unconscious mind will fill in those details based on expectation.[6]

5. Mlodinow, at 33.
6. Mlodinow, at 62.

All of this shows that our minds work on expectations. And knowing that, and by using your conscious mind, you can change your expectations for your unconscious mind. To see how this works, consider how memory not only records but creates.

As you repeat the process of recalling an event, with your unconscious mind filling in the gaps, you stop recalling the actual event and instead recall the "memory" created by your mind. In other words, as you reinforce these "memories" over time, you will believe these memories of memories as though they are the *real* memories. That is, your mind cannot tell the difference between a real memory from a vividly imagined one. That means that you could just make one up, and after enough time, if you repeatedly and vividly remember it, you would eventually believe that memory was real because the nervous system cannot tell the difference between real or imagined experiences.[7]

In the same way, you can set your unconscious expectation about your performance, which will ultimately influence the way it performs subconsciously during times of stress. Unconscious performance starts with an expectation about the self. The view you hold of yourself is made up from a system of ideas you hold about yourself. Some of those are positive and some are negative. Your unconscious self has no preference whether you have a positive or negative view of your abilities—it has just one goal: consistency. Consistent ideas are accepted and inconsistent ones are rejected.[8] This means that your mind accepts ideas that conform with your expectations and rejects those ideas that do not, and it fills in gaps based on your expectation. So, when you are performing and your mental scripts kick in to help you, it will perform in a manner consistent with your expectation. As such, whether you think you will succeed or fail, your unconscious script will push you in that direction.

In other words, if you think you are skilled at some ability, you will reject thoughts and experiences that tend to show otherwise, and accept those that reinforce your skills. On the other hand, if you believe you are unskilled, your mind will emphasize those experiences that reinforce your failures. Simply put, if you think something is hard, you will tend to emphasize those parts of it that are hard, and thus, it will actually be harder. But, if you tend to think something is easy or you are capable of doing it, you will tend to highlight those things that confirm that belief. All of that will have an actual, real-world influence on your performance.

---

7. Mlodinow, at 66, 74; Maxwell Maltz, *Psycho-Cybernetics*, at 32 (1960).
8. Maltz, at 4, 70.

All of this confirms what most people know intuitively; whether you think you can or you think you can't, you are right.

B. Cultivating the Right Mental Framework

You need to do more than just think positively. It takes work to create positive frameworks and train your brain to fill in the gaps with positive expectations. One of the easiest and most basic training you can do for your brain is vivid memory exercises.

Recall that your conscious can influence your unconscious. And recall how our mind cannot tell a real memory from a vividly remembered one. You could make one up, and eventually truthfully believe it.[9] You can use those concepts to create the self-image you want, which will, in turn, support your goals. To do so, you should vividly picture the goals you want to achieve or the abilities you want to have. Picture yourself reading and understanding. Picture yourself in class understanding the material and performing the way you want. Picture yourself sitting at an exam, reading the prompt, and writing the exam without difficulty. See the room; feel the pen (or computer keys); become familiar with the feeling that you can do it. The more detailed you make the memories, the more vivid they will become, and the more your brain will mistake them for actual memories. During a real exam, when stress kicks in and your automated scripts take over, these fake experiences will support you during the real one.

Studies have shown that mental imaging techniques can actually improve performance when combined with actual practice.[10] So, while real practice makes perfect, mental practice can also help. Mental practice will allow you to develop an intuition, an unconscious mental script, that will allow you to act quickly in new situations and respond in the way you want.[11] By creating a self-image, goals, and memories that conform with how you want the world to be, you will create a situation where you will act accordingly when the situation arises.

Many students complain about and focus on the difficulties of law school. They complain about the workload, the professors, the cases, the schedule, the exams, and anything else that is not immediately comprehensible. That focus is unhelpful. These negative thoughts can become expectations that, in turn, become goals that their unconscious mind will work towards. And they will succeed in fulfilling those goals. They will confirm their expectations that

---

9. Mlodinow, at 66, 74.
10. Thagard, at 103.
11. Kahneman, at 12.

the cases are difficult to read, that class is boring, and that exams are difficult. Instead of operating toward the goals they want (success and understanding), their mind will unconsciously work toward their expectations (difficulty and failure) and they will struggle because their minds are steering them toward their expectations.

Sure, law school is difficult and no magical thinking will change that. But the way you approach your studies—your expectations about it—can help change the way you process information on a daily basis. Go in with the right expectations and the material will become second nature. It will become easier to understand. Your unconscious mind will automate the techniques you learn in this book, creating skills that will automate the process. Rather than forcing yourself to overcome something that you've convinced yourself is difficult, you can trust yourself to succeed. In times of stress, your subconscious can either help you succeed or it can help you fail. So program it to succeed.

II. Logic Frameworks

Logic is the foundation of all law. You do not need to be a logician to do well in law school, but you do need to be fluent in basic logic. If you can master a few basic concepts and apply them, then you will be ready for anything law school throws at you.

A. Arguments

Law school is about arguments. Reading them, listening to them, evaluating them, and making your own. Ultimately, your success on exams will depend on your ability to write arguments quickly and coherently. You will be graded on your arguments, pure and simple. Same thing when you actually practice law. You win or lose based on your arguments. So, let's start by looking at what an argument is (and what it is not).

An argument is not two people yelling at each other. It is not two people expressing a different opinion. In fact, an argument does not even require two opposing points of view. An explanation of facts is also not an argument. An argument is more like a mathematical proof that justifies a conclusion. Technically, it is a "group of statements, one or more of which (the premises) are claimed to provide support for, or reasons to believe, one of the others (the conclusions)."[12] In other words, an argument gives reasons to support a conclusion.

In law school, the "premises" are the legal rules (major premises) and the facts (minor premises). Arguments are good when the conclusion naturally flows from the premises—when the rule and facts compel the conclusion. If the conclusion *must* follow from the premises, then it is called a deductive argument. If the conclusion *probably* follows from the premises, then it is called inductive. Both types of arguments can be equally effective. And while you will never need to identify whether an argument is deductive or inductive in law school (or beyond), it is helpful to understand the difference because it determines how you phrase your conclusions.

A deductive argument means that the conclusion *must* be true if the premises are true. Feed a deductive argument true statements and a true conclusion will always follow. For example:

- all men are mortal (major premise or rule);
- Socrates is a man (minor premise or fact);
- therefore, Socrates is a mortal (conclusion).

If those premises are true (all men are mortal, and Socrates is a man), then the conclusion *must* be true (Socrates *must be* a mortal). There is no question about the conclusion with those premises. And as a result, you can say without reservation that Socrates *is* a mortal. There is no doubt and there is no need to qualify your conclusion.

In law school, when you have a legal rule made up of conjunctive elements that must all be satisfied, your argument will be deductive. Conjunctive elements use the word *and* rather than the word *or*. An element-rule will contain several premises that must all exist for the rule to be satisfied. To make a deductive argument, you start with the rule statement (the elements), add the facts, and conclude.

For example, to satisfy the statute of frauds in a contract for real property there are two elements, the agreement must be (1) in writing *and* (2) signed. Both elements must be satisfied. Once we plug in the facts, for example, Darren signed a written contract to buy Polly's home, there is no question that the conclusion is true that Darren and Polly's contract satisfied the statute of frauds.

An inductive argument, on the other hand, involves probabilistic reasoning. That means the conclusion will likely, probably, or possibly be true if the premises are true. It can be that the conclusion is very likely true or even almost im-

12. Patrick J. Hurley, *A Concise Introduction to Logic*, at 1 (2008).

possible to be false, but if there is some possibility, any possibility, that the conclusion is not true (even if all premises are true), then the argument is inductive. And that influences how you frame your conclusion; instead of a definitive conclusion, it will be a probabilistic one. For example, if we change the premises above to *most* men are mortal (just assume that is true) and Socrates is a man, then you would say that it is *likely* that Socrates is a mortal. You could not conclude that Socrates *is* a mortal, like above, because now there is a possibility (however small) that he is not.

In law school, you will use inductive reasoning when you have a disjunctive set of factors or elements of a rule. This generally occurs when a number of conditions are weighed together to satisfy a rule. For example, in employment law, there is a distinction between an employee and an independent contractor. There is no set of elements that distinguishes an employee from an independent contractor. Instead, there are a number of factors that a court considers: (a) the amount of control by the employer over the employee; (b) the duration of relationship; (c) who provides the equipment; (d) compensation and benefits; and, (e) discipline. The more these factors tend to show employer control, the more likely the conclusion that the person is an employee rather than an independent contractor. Thus, if most of those factors are present, you would conclude in a manner reflecting that probability. You would not say that it is certain that this person will be found to be an employee; instead, you would say, this person is *likely* an employee, or there is *strong* evidence that this person is an employee.

Some indicator words for inductive conclusions include: probably, improbably, plausible, implausible, likely, unlikely, and reasonable to conclude.[13]

B. Syllogisms

Whether conjunctive or disjunctive, legal arguments follow a pattern. That pattern is called a syllogism. Syllogisms are the foundation of all legal reasoning.[14] As discussed above, logic is like a mathematical proof and a syllogism is its basic form; A plus B equals C. The *A* is the major premise, which is the legal rule. The *B* is the minor premise, which is the facts. And the *C* is the conclusion. So, what you have in a legal argument is: a rule plus facts equal a conclusion. In law school, you will hear this described as IRAC (issue, rule, application, conclusions), which we will discuss in detail later.

---

13. Hurley, at 32.

14. Antonin Scalia & Bryan A. Garner, *Making Your Case: The Art of Persuading Judges*, at 41 (2008); Bryan A. Garner, *The Winning Brief*, at 111 (3d ed.) (2014); Richard A. Posner, *How Judges Think*, at 41 (2008).

Recall the Socrates argument, which is the classic example of a syllogism. Let's break that down. What we have in the Socrates syllogism is:

- all men are mortal (rule-premise);
- Socrates is a man (fact-premise);
- therefore, Socrates is mortal (conclusion).

In an IRAC form, you add the issue or question upfront: The issue is whether Socrates is a mortal (I). The rule is that all men are mortal (R). Socrates is a man (A). Therefore, Socrates is mortal (C).

Generally for legal arguments, however, a three-line syllogism will not cut it. Legal arguments require syllogisms upon syllogisms. You start with a legal rule that contains multiple elements that need to be defined, which become more rules, and each element is then analyzed itself. So, what happens is that your rule statement will need to be broken down into syllogisms themselves. Each time you explain or define an element or factor, you set up a new syllogism. If you can follow that form you will nail any test. All that is left is identifying what rule you need for the facts you are given. The rest simply follows that form.

For example, to answer a question of whether the parties entered a contract you have a three-element rule, there must be: (1) an offer, (2) consideration, and (3) acceptance. That is your major rule statement. Then, you need to analyze each element by breaking that down into its own syllogism. For example, you need to create a syllogism to define the first element of *offer* and then plug in the facts to reach a conclusion as to that element. Thus, you would create a new syllogism explaining that an offer exists where there is a manifestation of intention to be bound to a contract (rule).[15] You then plug in your fact-premise, which for example could be: the defendant told the plaintiff he wanted to sell him five widgets for twenty-five dollars (facts). And finally, you conclude: therefore, the defendant manifested an intent to be bound to a contract. You would then do the same for each element in the series. Then do that again for minority rules or defenses.

---

15. In practice, this gets even more complicated because you can break down that subrule into more subrules. In particular, to determine whether one has "manifested an intent to be bound," there is a set of factors to consider. To determine whether the facts satisfy that subrule, you set up another syllogism. "To establish the intent to be bound, courts look at the following...." Then you plug in the facts and conclude. You can see how this rabbit-hole can keep going. Part of your skill and success on exams will be how you can accurately and quickly break these elements into their subelements, analyze them, and make it all readable.

Conditional statements may also be used for rule statements. A conditional statement is an *if-then* statement; for example, if it rains then the ground is wet.[16] For a legal application, consider the elements for common law burglary, which are: the breaking and entering of the dwelling of another at night with the intent to commit a felony inside. There are multiple elements there: breaking, entering, dwelling, of another, at night, and intent to commit a felony inside. Start with the element *dwelling*. A dwelling is defined as somewhere a person regularly sleeps. Instead of saying it that way, you could write your rule statement as a conditional statement: *If* it is somewhere a person regularly sleeps *then* it is a dwelling (R). This is the same as "a dwelling is a place where a person regularly sleeps." Either way is fine. Using a conditional is just another way of writing the rule.

As you can see, every law is just a rule statement that needs to be broken down and defined. And there are subrules within those rules. You need to identify the rule and the parts of the rule that get further definitions. The more you can break it down, the better your analysis. As discussed later, the best way to do well on an exam is simply to be able to quickly break down a rule into its components. The further you can break it, the more points you can get. Once you set out the law, it is a simple matter of plugging in the facts to the rule.

C. Analogies

Another important tool is analogical reasoning. Analogies compare similarities between different things. An analogical argument is structured like this: Case X has qualities a, b, c, and z; Case Y has qualities a, b, and c; therefore, Case Y also has quality z. The strength of that argument depends on whether the qualities a, b, and c are connected in some meaningful way to z.[17] When arguing against the analogy, you would point out the relevant differences between X and Y.

Lawyers often use analogical reasoning to argue for certain outcomes. For example, a lawyer may say: The issue is whether my client should win (I); Case

---

16. It is important to note that you cannot simply switch the if and then portions. So, while it is always true that every time it rains the exposed ground will be wet, it is not always true that every time the exposed ground is wet it rained; someone could have sprayed water with a hose or dropped a bucket of water. What you can do is switch the if and then conditions and negate them. In other words, you could say, if the exposed ground is not wet then it did not rain. That will always be true. You will always know that if the exposed ground is dry, then it did not rain.

17. Hurley, at 468.

X has qualities a, b, c, and it won (R); my case has qualities a, b, and c (A); therefore, we should win too (C). As you can see, even analogies use the same argument formula (I-R-A-C).

Analogical reasoning is only important when you are comparing cases; something you will do while discussing cases in class and in your writing classes (and later when you actually practice). You generally do not need to do this in exams, however.[18] A law school exam will present you with facts. Your job will be to spot the legal issue, identify the rule, apply the relevant facts, and conclude. You will almost *never* analogize the facts to a case you read in class. You just don't need to, and it won't get you far. There is too little time in a law school exam to do more than apply the facts you are given to the rules, minority rules, and defenses. And what's more, you will not be expected to.

D. Fallacies

A fallacy is a defective argument. They are based on faulty reasoning, misleading, or unsound arguments. Many of them are so common they follow familiar forms. It is good to know some common logical fallacies so that you avoid them, but there is no need to study them and know them all by name. It is good enough to be able to point out *why* the reasoning is wrong, rather than to identify the fallacy by name. In other words, instead of saying that your opponent has committed the fallacy of *post hoc ergo propter hoc*, you may simply say that my opponent thinks that just because X happened before Y, X caused Y, and then point out why that is wrong.

Here are some examples broken down by fallacy type.

1. Relevance

One category of fallacies are fallacies of relevance. Fallacies of relevance involve logically irrelevant premises. The most common ones you may confront in law school (and beyond) are strawmen and red herrings.

A strawman distorts an argument for the purpose of more easily attacking it, and then concludes that the real argument has been defeated. It is called a "strawman," because one sets up a strawman, knocks it down, and then concludes that the real argument is knocked over too. When someone creates a

18. *Generally*, of course, because there could be times you need to. It depends on the professor. As discussed later, a good way to determine whether you need to discuss cases on exams is to review old exams and check with other students. Also, as discussed later, sometimes professors steal the basic facts and issues from cases and simply repurpose them with new facts. In instances where it is clear, you could cite the case in an answer.

strawman, they are taking someone else's words out of context or distorting the position and then attacking that distorted position as if that was the opponent's position. A strawman often exaggerates the position to make it seem more extreme and then knocks down that exaggerated position.

A red herring is intended to lead the reader or listener off track. A red herring diverts attention by subtly changing the subject, then draws a conclusion about that changed subject rather than the actual subject.[19] The key difference between a strawman and red herring is that the red herring involves a change in the subject, rather than a distortion.

For example, compare a strawman and red herring in similar arguments. Let's say Mr. X argues we should have stricter gun control measures including mental health screening. A strawman may say in response, Mr. X is trying to take all our guns away and we need guns to protect ourselves. But Mr. X said nothing about taking all our guns away; instead, the arguer distorted or exaggerated the argument and then knocked that argument down. A red herring, in contrast, may reply in response to the gun-control argument that people are harmed with cars, knives, and hammers every day, so why don't you take those away. While we might want to address cars, knives and hammers, those have nothing to do with whether we need stricter gun controls.

2. Fallacies of Weak Induction

Another category of fallacies are fallacies of weak induction. Fallacies of weak induction relate to the strength of the connection between the premises and conclusion. In this type of fallacy, there is typically only a shred of evidence for the conclusion, but it is nowhere near strong enough to have a reasonable person believe the conclusion. Often, it contains an emotional element.

A weak analogy is a common fallacy of weak induction. This occurs when the similarities in the comparison are not strong.

A slippery slope is often used in the law and politics. In law, it is sometimes referred to as a "parade of horribles." The fallacy occurs when the conclusion rests on a number of chain reactions and there is not sufficient reason to think the chains will actually occur.[20] But keep in mind that a parade of horribles is not a fallacy if the events are actually likely to occur. It is only a fallacy when those consequences are unlikely.

In the appeal to ignorance, the arguer states that nothing has been proven about a thing, but then makes a definite conclusion about that same thing. For example, nobody has shown that X is true, and therefore X is false. But this

19. Hurley, at 123, 125.
20. Hurley, at 139.

line of reasoning is not a fallacy if one would expect there to be evidence of X and there is no evidence of X. If that occurs, one can reasonably conclude that evidence of X likely does not exist. That conclusion is inductive and its strength depends on how much research has been done and the likelihood one would find evidence.

A hasty generalization occurs when one draws a conclusion about a group from evidence that pertains to only a selected sample (stereotypes). Again, be careful because this is not a fallacy when there is a reasonable likelihood that the sample is actually representative of the group (a scientific sample).

3. Fallacies of Presumption

Fallacies of presumption occur when the premises presume what they are trying to prove. An example is begging the question, which occurs when one assumes what they want to prove and then tries to prove it.[21] It is the same as circular reasoning. This may go something like this: "I'm a good student, so you should give me an A." That begs the question as to whether you are a good student because it assumes that you are a good student. The phrase begging the question does not mean, however, "raising a question." Think back to the gun-control example: if one argues that we should have stricter gun-control, one might say in response that this argument begs the question whether we should abolish the second amendment. It doesn't. What the responder is saying is that this *raises* the question whether we should abolish the second amendment. Whether that does or does not is another question, but it is not technically begging the question.

Another fallacy of presumption is the false dichotomy, which occurs when a disjunctive premise (either, or) presents two alternatives as the only two alternatives. It is a fallacy when there are more than two choices. Similarly, beware of complex questions, including the infamous loaded question, "When did you stop drinking?" That assumes, of course, that you had been drinking.

These are just a handful of examples that come up in the law. You will undoubtedly see many others.

---

21. A related, but perfectly acceptable, argument is one that implies a commonly known premise. A syllogism that leaves out an implied major premise is called an *enthymeme*. For example, a major premise for a breach of contract case is that a contract requires consideration (rule statement). An arguer may at times leave out that rule statement and instead have a complete argument consisting of: X did not provide consideration (rule and application), and therefore, there is no contract (conclusion). Scalia & Garner, at 87. As a law student in exams and papers, however, you should not use enthymemes. Regardless of how basic you think the proposition is, you must show your work on papers and exams (especially exams).

E. Logic Connectors

Before we leave logic, let's look at a few tricky logic connectors that are often misused in law: *ambiguous v. vague*, *necessary v. sufficient*, and *only*.

Ambiguous v. *vague*. When someone says something is ambiguous it means the statement is susceptible of multiple meanings. For example, if I said a margarita is a cool drink, the word "cool" is ambiguous because it could mean that it is cold or fashionable. When something is ambiguous, you can resolve the problem by picking a definition. When someone says something is vague it means that the boundaries are not defined. For example, if I said, I'll be back later, the word "later" is vague because you don't know exactly when I'll be back. You can resolve vagueness by defining the boundaries.

Necessary v. Sufficient. A necessary condition is one that *must* exist for the conclusion to exist. A sufficient condition is one of many conditions that can exist to trigger the conclusion. For example, having gas in your car is a necessary condition for a car to start. Without gas, the car will not start. It is necessary. While there are many other things needed for your car to start, without gas, it won't happen. An example of a sufficient condition is, if it rains the ground will be wet. Raining is a sufficient condition to make the ground wet, but it does not have to occur to make the ground wet. A sprinkler could have made the ground wet as well.

Only. The word *only* means "alone," "solely," and "no other," and it can typically be put in any place of a sentence. Indeed, where the word *only* is placed in a sentence can radically change its meaning. The best way to avoid confusion is to put the word *only* right before the word you want to modify. A great example of the many ways *only* can cause confusion depending on placement is with the sentence: "the butler says he saw the murder." If you put *only* in almost any point of that sentence you can change its meaning. "Only the butler says he saw the murder" (just the butler saw it); "The butler only says he saw the murder" (the butler says, but cannot prove, he saw it); "the butler says only he saw the murder" (the butler says that he alone saw the murder); "the butler says he only saw the murder" (he saw it, but did not hear it); "the butler says he saw only the murder" (the butler saw solely the murder but nothing else).[22]

* * *

22. Patricia T. O'Conner, *Woe Is I: The Grammarphobe's Guide to Better English in Plain English*, at 122 (2009) (3d ed.).

From here we move on to the substance. But, before we do, it is important to pause and consider again just how important these first two frameworks are for success. No matter what you do in law school, or hope to do beyond, you need to approach it with the right attitude and foundation. It goes without saying that law school will be stressful, and when that happens, you will need to fall back on your automated systems. If those automated systems are ready for the task ahead, then you will find yourself much better equipped to succeed. Couple that with a strong foundation in basic logic, and you will be ready to analyze and answer any question.

CHAPTER TWO

Class Frameworks

There are essentially two important skills for class: preparation and participation. As you read through this chapter, you will see that the preparation portion of this chapter is longer and more detailed than the participation portion. The reason is that preparation is key to excelling in class, and participation follows from preparation. It is also fundamental to your success as a law student. Law school classes are not just lectures; they are discussions that you are expected to participate in. To do so, you must be prepared. Once you do that, the participation part is easy.

I. Preparation

A. How to Read

Preparation is reading. You probably didn't think you would have to study how to read, but you do. Reading is a skill. You can be good at it, or you can be bad at it. And for lawyers, reading is a critical skill because lawyers are basically professional readers and writers. The work a lawyer does depends on their ability to read, understand, and interpret text. It is the same for law students. Your reading and interpretation skills are critical to your grade because they influence how quickly you can process and write on an exam.

The skill of reading is measured by understanding. You are not reading for information; you are reading for understanding. There is a difference. Reading for information requires a comprehension of the *what* only. Reading for understanding, however, requires comprehension of both the *what* and the *why*. Another way to think about it is that understanding is measured by your ability to receive the information the writer intended to communicate.[1] When you begin reading you start at an unequal level of knowledge with the writer. Your first task of understanding, then, is to overcome that knowledge inequity by "approaching equality with the writer."[2] Note that you "*approach* equality," which means that you may never achieve it. But that is ok. You don't need to reach full equality with the writer. The key to understanding is moving along the spectrum from no understanding to full understanding. The skill of reading is measured by your ability to get as far along that spectrum as you can.

It is therefore imperative to understand, rather than to simply read, the cases. Understanding the cases is important for your ability to extract the key legal principles from the case, which is discussed in more detail below. But understanding the cases has other benefits as well. First, the cases you read demonstrate winning arguments. By dissecting the cases you read, you are learning better argument techniques and will become better at crafting your own arguments. Second, those cases preview fact patterns you may see in your exams. Often, cases are chosen for law school textbooks because they are illustrative of a principle with uncomplicated facts. United States Supreme Court cases are often particularly illustrative of this phenomenon. The cases that get to the United States Supreme Court typically have a simple fact pattern that allows the Justices to explain a rule of general application. For that same reason, the cases you read contain examples of fact patterns that professors can use to design your tests. And, to be sure, your professors will pull from those fact patterns. So, the more you understand those facts, the better prepared you will be to spot them on an exam.

The problem with some law students is that they do not understand the cases. And, by that, I don't mean that they are incapable; they simply do not take the time to do so. They want the *what* by having a black-letter legal rule handed to them, but they don't want to take the time to understand the *why*. They expect the teacher to tell them the what and the why of a case. But law professors don't do that, which causes students to become disappointed and frustrated. What these students fail to do is look to the case for answers. You must ask the case questions you would ask your professor. The answers are there—you just have to find them.[3] It is your job as a law student to find the

---

1. Mortimer J. Adler & Charles Van Doren, *How to Read a Book: The Classic Guide to Intelligent Reading*, at 7 (1972) (2d ed.).

2. Adler & Doren, at 10.

3. Sometimes the answers are not in the case. But knowing that the answer is *not* there takes the same amount of work (or more) as knowing that the answer *is* there. You must fully understand the case to be able to say, "the case does not answer X." Only when you

answer, and it will be your job as a lawyer to do so as well.[4] When you can answer your questions from the writing itself, you understand it. Remember that law school is more like self-guided study rather than school in the traditional sense of providing you with information that you repeat. Of course, some professors will teach you in a traditional sense of showing. They will explain the what and give you the legal rules. Those are valuable classes, and you can get mediocre grades by just listening. You can do the same in classes where the professor does not give you the answers. You can find outlines and hornbooks that provide all the answers you need at your fingertips. That will get you by. But the point of this book is not to just get by, it is to succeed. That requires understanding.

B. The Parts of a Case

Before we discuss how to understand a case, you should be familiar with the parts of a legal opinion (a case). Part of your task in reading a case will be to break it into its components. Almost every opinion contains these parts:

Issue. The issue is the question the court must resolve. Issues usually start with *whether*. For example, "whether the parties formed a contract." Sometimes a court just states the parties' arguments: the plaintiff claims X and the defendant claims Y. Usually these are mirror images and represent the issue for the court. The issue usually comes up front, but in older cases, it sometimes comes after the facts.

Facts. In a well-written case, the only facts you will find are those that matter to the conclusion. In others you will find unnecessary facts. Disregard them. The only important facts are those that affect the holding. You will know which facts are the important ones because they will be discussed during the court's application of the legal rules to the facts.

---

truly understand the case can you say that it is missing something. This is an important skill for your career beyond law school as well. In real life cases, there is always missing information. A good lawyer can spot that missing information and point it out. But, again, to say something is missing requires careful review.

4. When you are a practicing lawyer, you will need to figure out something new every day. That is the job. You will almost never know the answer to a question. The best thing you can do is spot the issue and know where to find the framework to give an answer. Then you have to analyze the facts against that framework. In this way, law school approaches practice. And as an associate first leaving law school, partners will expect you to figure things out. It's what they pay you for.

Rules. The legal rules, of course, are the rules that the court will apply against the facts to determine the holding. In terms of syllogisms discussed in Chapter 1, it is the major premise.

Application. The application is the court's reasoning. You will know it when you see it because the court is plugging the facts into the legal rule. It is the minor-premise of the syllogism.

Holding. A holding is a special type of conclusion. A conclusion sums up an argument. It is the result of the application of the facts to the rule. But a conclusion is only a *holding* when that conclusion is required to resolve the case.

To understand this, consider non-holdings—what lawyers call *dicta*. Dicta is a conclusion that the court does not need to reach. For example, a legal rule may include a threshold element—an element that must be satisfied before other elements are discussed—but the court may find that this threshold element has not been satisfied, and thus the case is over. If it does that, then the court does not need to discuss the other elements. But it may do so anyway. The court may say something like "even if that element was satisfied, the other elements are not satisfied because...." That sentence, and anything following it, is dicta. In another example, sometimes a court will comment on an argument that is not necessary to the holding. For instance, a party may make two arguments on why it satisfied a certain element. The court needs to only accept one. Once it does, it's discussion of the other argument is dicta. Dicta can come in many forms, but the key in finding dicta is that it is not necessary to decide the case.

A holding is also not the legal rule the court sets out in defining how it will determine the case. The holding is the application of that rule to the facts of a case. For example, a court does not hold that a contract requires three elements; that is the legal rule. There are times, however, usually in appellate courts, when the dispute *is* over what legal rule applies. The court will identify the issue as whether such and such rule applies, and then discuss what legal rule applies. It will then conclude that the rule that applies was correct or should be something else. In that case, that conclusion will be the holding. Again, the important point in finding the holding is to find the question the court is answering.

Finally, be mindful of the words you use to describe what a court is doing. Courts do not "believe" or "think." A court "holds," "decides," "finds" (facts), and "concludes." Use the right word when you are describing the court's actions.

C. Understanding a Case

Understanding is a process. The best way to understand a case is to read it in three steps: (1) skim it; (2) read it once through; and then (3), read it again, analytically. This will take time in the beginning, but later it will become second nature and you can truncate (if not skip) the first two steps. But, in the beginning, it is important to your success that you follow each step. There are two reasons that you should not skip steps in the beginning. *First*, the cases you read in your first-year classes will be in classic legal subjects, and those cases can go back centuries. That means that some of them are nearly incomprehensible. The language is dense and they are not organized like a modern opinion. The three-step process will help you understand those cases. *Second*, as a general principle, you are still learning and so even modern cases will be difficult to read at first. As you get more experience it will become easier as you recognize patterns and become familiar with the writing style. But in the beginning it will be a challenge.

1. Skim It

The first step in reading a case is to skim it. While skimming, you want to identify the parts of the case. In some opinions (more modern ones), there will be headings and subheadings that provide a roadmap of each part of the case. In other opinions, there may not be headings to guide you, but you will usually be able to pick out these parts by looking at the first or last sentences of a paragraph (and you will begin to appreciate better writing that includes indicator words as discussed in Chapter 3).

What you really want to find in your initial skim is the issue and the holding. Knowing what the court needs to decide and what it ultimately decided will key you into what you need to focus on in your second and third full reads. The issue or issues will typically be found up front in the first paragraph or so. In the beginning paragraphs, the court may discuss the procedural posture of the case, who the parties are, and what the court needs to decide (the issue). Many times, there is more than one issue, and issue statements may be scattered throughout the opinion. But, typically, each sub-issue statement will precede its own argument, including the rule, application, and holding. Sometimes there will be no issue statement, or you may not find it in your skim. That is why you always look for the holding, which is a useful way of identifying the issue. The holding will always answer the issue.

While you skim, also take note of any unusual terms that are repeated throughout the opinion that seem important. Again, these terms may be important ones and will focus your attention on understanding them while you move through your second and third full reads.

2. Read It

The second step is a full read through. Just read it. No highlighting, marking, or rereading. Read the whole opinion once through without stopping. Don't get lost trying to understand all the fine points, that is what the final reading is for. You will get an understanding of the whole this way, and will be better prepared to understand the finer points on your analytical read.

3. Analyze It

The third step is a full, analytical reading. This is where the real work is done and you move along the spectrum toward understanding. To truly understand the case, you must be active and invested—you must engage with the text.

Active reading requires you to annotate in the text. That means writing in it if you are reading on paper or annotating with digital tools while reading digitally. Indeed, the mere act of reading with a pen and writing in the text aids your understanding by activating different parts of your brain. It is one thing for your brain to read something (that activates a certain portion of the brain), but it is another to read something and physically engage with it (that activates another). Studies show that the simple act of holding a pen and writing in a book activates more of your brain, which aids understanding.[5]

Additionally, the act of writing in the book creates a mental map of the page that aids understanding. Marking up text on a page creates a visual picture that your memory can access, rather than just a wall of words on a page.[6] Creating a mental map allows for faster recall in both remembering and reviewing text. When you create a mental map and you re-review the text, it helps you find the information in the text faster. In other words, the addition of your personal marks creates physical landmarks in the text that allows you to find the information you are looking for faster.

---

5. Jude Nicholas, *From active touch to tactile communication: What's tactile cognition got to do with it?*, *available at* https://tinyurl.com/ActivetoTactileCommunication.

6. Ferris Jabr, *The Reading Brain in the Digital Age: The Science of Paper versus Screens* (April 11, 2013), *available at* https://tinyurl.com/TheReadingBrain.

It is important to work with a pen not a highlighter. Writing with a pen allows you to use a range of marks and words that are helpful to aid your understanding. Several differently colored highlighters may allow you to identify the different portions of an opinion, but it will not allow you to do the interactive work that a pen does.[7] Using a pen allows you to draw circles, boxes, brackets, underlines, asterisks, stars, slashes, or any other mark that you are comfortable with. It also allows you to write in the margins, which is the most important step. Whatever marks you like, use them in a consistent manner. In other words, if you use a box for a conclusion or thesis of a paragraph, always do that. If you use a circle for a key term, always do that. If you use underlining for reasoning, always do that. Whatever you choose, formulate a system that you will use in your reading throughout school. That way, when you go back later, you will be able to *see* the structure of a paragraph instantly without re-reading it.

As mentioned, it is important to write in the margins. You will write two basic categories of information in the margins: (1) the portion of the case the paragraph relates to; and (2) a summary of the paragraph in your own words. So, next to a paragraph (or a group of paragraphs) explaining the facts, you might write *facts* next to the start of that section and circle it or underline it, or whatever mark you choose. These serve as headings in the margin that you can easily find, and also will help create the visual map of the opinion. Additionally, you should write a summary of the paragraph in the margin. It can be one word or a sentence or two—not much more—you are not rewriting the paragraph, that would be pointless. What you want to do is explain the paragraph as simply as possible. Just reduce the paragraph to a simple statement. You write the paragraph's thesis, it's conclusion, a description of the key facts in it, or legal rule in the margin. What you are doing here is the final step in understanding. By summing up the point of the paragraph in a simple statement, *in your own words*, you are demonstrating that you understand it.[8] If you can rewrite the point of the paragraph in your own words, you are approaching equal understanding with the writer. Remember it must be in your own words. If you are merely copying the text, you are not demonstrating your understanding of the message. Summarizing it in

7. I am not against using different colors to differentiate the sections of the opinion. In fact, I think doing so can help your mental map and overall understanding. When I was in law school, I used one of those pens with four different colors that you could switch between. The important point is to use something that allows you to create the different types of marks and then write in the margins to summarize your understanding.

8. Adler & Doren, at 125.

your own words forces you to truly understand. You may think you understand something you read, but when you try to sum it up, you might be unable to. "The person who says he knows what he thinks but cannot express it usually does not know what he thinks."[9] When you can sum it up, you understand it. This process has the added bonus of reinforcing the neural connections necessary to make a memory, as you are not just understanding it, but recreating it in your own words.

The following is an example of a famous case you may see in your contracts course, *Hadley v. Baxendale.* It addresses a rule relating to measuring foreseeable damages when a party breaches a contract. This case is old, difficult to read, but relatively simple in principle. It is a rule that many state courts follow to this day. And it is a good example of how applying the principles we've discussed can help you understand a case.

9. Adler & Doren, at 49.

Hadley v Baxendale
9 Exch. 341, 156 Eng.Rep. 145.
(Court of Exchequer, 1854)

Facts

At the trial before Crompton, J., at the last Gloucester Assizes, it appeared that the plaintiffs carried on an extensive business as millers at Gloucester; and that on the 11th on May, their mill was stopped by a breakage of the crank shaft by which the mill was worked. The steam-engine was manufactured by Messrs. Joyce & Co., the engineers, at Greenwich, and it became necessary to send the shaft as a pattern for a new one to Greenwich. The fracture was discovered on the 12th, and on the 13th the plaintiffs sent one of their servants to the office of the defendants, who are the well-known carriers trading under the name of Pickford & Co., for the purpose of having the shaft carried to Greenwich. The plaintiffs' servant told the clerk that the mill was stopped, and that the shaft must be sent immediately; and in answer to the inquiry when the shaft would be taken, the answer was, that if it was sent up by twelve o'clock any day, it would be delivered at Greenwich on the following day. On the following day the shaft was taken by the defendants, before noon, for the purpose of being conveyed to Greenwich, and the sum of 2l. 4s. was paid for its carriage for the whole distance; at the same time the defendants' clerk was told that a special entry, if required, should be made to hasten its delivery. The delivery of the shaft at Greenwich was delayed by some neglect; and the consequence was, that the plaintiffs did not receive the new shaft for several days after they would otherwise have done, and the working of their mill was thereby delayed, and they thereby lost the profits they would otherwise have received.

P contracted with D to send a broken part to be fixed. The delivery was late. P lost profit.

Issue

On the part of the defendants, it was objected that these damages were too remote, and that the defendants were not liable with respect to them. The learned Judge left the case generally to the jury, who found a verdict with £25 damages beyond the amount paid into Court.

Are lost profits available

Whateley, in last Michaelmas Term, obtained a rule nisi for a new trial, on the ground of misdirection.

Alderson, B. We think that there ought to be a new trial in this case; but, in so doing, we deem it to be expedient and necessary to state explicitly the rule which the Judge, at the next trial, ought, in our opinion, to direct the jury to be governed by when they estimate the damages.

It is, indeed, of the last importance that we should do this; for, if the jury are left without any definite rule to guide them, it will, in such cases as these, manifestly lead to the greatest injustice. The Courts have done this on several occasions; and, in Blake v. Midland Railway Company, 18 Q.B. 93, the Court granted a new trial on this very ground, that the rule had not been definitely laid down to the jury by the learned Judge at Nisi Prius.

"There are certain established rules," this Court says, in Alder v. Keighley, 15 M. & W. 117,"according to which the jury ought to find." And the Court, in that case, adds: "and here there is a clear rule, that the amount which would have been received if the contract had been kept, is the measure of damages if the contract is broken."

Now we think the proper rule in such a case as the present is this:-- Where two parties have made a contract which one of them has broken, the damages which the other party ought to receive in respect of such breach of contract should be such as may fairly and reasonably be considered either arising naturally, i.e., according to the usual course of things, from such breach of contract itself, or such as may reasonably be supposed to have been in the contemplation of both parties, at the time they made the contract, as the probable result of the breach of it. Now, if the special circumstances under which the contract was actually made were communicated by the plaintiffs to the defendants, and thus known to both parties, the damages resulting from the breach of such a contract, which they would reasonably contemplate, would be the amount of injury which would ordinarily follow from a breach of contract under these special circumstances so known and communicated. But, on the other hand, if these special circumstances were wholly unknown to the party breaking the contract, he, at the most, could only be supposed to have had in his contemplation the amount of injury which would arise generally, and in the great multitude of cases not affected by any special circumstances, from such a breach of contract. For, had the special circumstances been known, the parties might have specially provided for the breach of contract by special terms as to the damages in that case; and of this advantage it would be very unjust to deprive them. Now the above principles are those by which we think the jury ought to be guided in estimating the damages arising out of any breach of contract. It is said, that other cases such as breaches of contract in the nonpayment of money, or in the not making a good title of land, are to be treated as exceptions from this, and as governed by a conventional rule. But as, in such cases, both parties must be supposed to be cognizant of that well-known rule, these cases may, we think, be more properly classed under the rule above enunciated as to cases under known special circumstances, because there both parties may reasonably be presumed to contemplate the estimation of the amount of damages according to the conventional rule. Now, in the present case, if we are to apply the principles above laid down, we find that the only circumstances here communicated by the plaintiffs to the defendants at the time of the contract was made, were, that the article to be carried was the broken shaft of a mill, and that the plaintiffs were the millers of the mill.

But how do these circumstances shew reasonably that the profits of the mill must be stopped by an unreasonable delay in the delivery of the broken shaft by the carrier to the third person? Suppose the plaintiffs had another shaft in their possession put up or putting up at the time, and that they only wished to send back the broken shaft to the engineer who made it; it is clear that this would be quite consistent with the above circumstances, and yet the unreasonable delay in the delivery would have no effect upon the intermediate profits of the mill. Or, again, suppose that, at the time of the delivery to the carrier, the machinery of the mill had been in other respects defective, then, also, the same results would follow. Here it is true that the shaft was actually sent back to serve as a model for the new one, and that the want of a new one was the only cause of the stoppage of the mill, and that the loss of profits really arose from not sending down the new shaft in proper time, and that this arose from the delay in delivering the broken one to serve as a model. But it is obvious that, in the great multitude of cases of millers sending off broken shafts to third persons by a carrier under ordinary circumstances, such consequences would not, in all probability, have occurred; and these special circumstances were here never communicated by the plaintiffs to the defendants. It follows therefore, that the loss of profits here cannot reasonably be considered such a consequence of the breach of contract as could have been fairly and reasonably contemplated by both the parties when they made this contract. For such loss would neither have flowed naturally from the breach of this contract in the great multitude of such cases occurring under ordinary circumstances, nor were the special circumstances, which, perhaps, would have made it a reasonable and natural consequence of such breach of contract, communicated to or known by the defendants. The Judge ought, therefore, to have told the jury that upon the facts then before them they ought not to take the loss of profits into consideration at all in estimating the damages. There must therefore be a new trial in this case.

Holding
lost profits from delivery not generally (1) foreseeable and no special (2) circumstances communicated

Rule absolute.

This process not only activates your brain in all these great ways, but it leaves you with a book-briefing of the case. Briefing a case is an important part of your class preparation, and it is the final step in class preparation. A book-brief is valuable because it helps you create a brief as you read. Later, as you cut some corners, that book-brief may be all you need.

To further prepare for class, you should write a full case brief for every case you read. A full case brief provides a single page summary of the opinion. Again, this reinforces your understanding, and also provides a quick reference for you in class (and will be helpful later when you start outlining). A full case brief includes all the parts of the case: the issue, key facts, the legal rule, the reasoning, and the holding. It can look however you want. The point is to create something that you can easily read. And if you create it, then you will be able to find the key information. There is no strict formula. The important thing is that *you* create it.

Here is a sample template for a case brief.

Case Name

- Parties
  - Plaintiff
  - Defendant
- Issues
  - Issue 1
  - Issue 2
- Facts
  - Issue 1
    - Key facts for issue 1
  - Issue 2
    - Key facts for issue 2
- Holdings
  - Issue 1
    - Reasoning
  - Issue 2
    - Reasoning

II. Participation

You may think that class is a time to sit back and learn the law—it's not. Class is not a passive activity where you will be given all the legal rules. It is an active discussion. You will be expected to participate. Your professors will ask you questions designed to test your understanding. You will be expected to recount the issues, facts, and holdings in the cases. What's more, you will be expected to understand the court's reasoning and explain it to the class. Your professors will ask questions to direct your focus and engage you in critical thinking. This is the Socratic method. It may sound like a law-school stereotype, but it still very much exists. To get anything out of the Socratic method, however, you must be prepared by the time you get to class. If you've done the steps we've discussed above, however, you will be more than prepared.[10] It is as simple as that.

A. Being Active in Class

Participation in class is an important tool you can use for understanding. Many students hate the way law school classes are taught and constantly complain about it. They want the rules handed to them. They think that they are paying all this money for school and that they should be spoon-fed the answers. But that is not how it works. Nor would it make you into a good lawyer. Being a good lawyer requires participation. It requires curiosity. It requires analysis. All of that requires action. And action requires participation.

Participation has other great benefits. *First*, you get to check your understanding. If you cannot answer a question, or answer it wrong, you can find out why. By participating, you test your understanding in real time. What you thought you understood may be different from what the professor wants you to see, and if so, you must see it from their perspective. You may think the point of the case is X, but the professor thinks it was Y. Whether the professor is right or wrong doesn't matter—the professor will expect Y on the exam.

Second, participation prepares you to think on your feet. This is crucial preparation for the exam. The professor will throw you curveballs and hypotheticals, and you will have the chance to test your understanding and ability to apply the rules to these new situations on the fly. No one else but the person answering the question gets the full benefit of this process. Sure, your fellow students can think of answers in their head at their desk, and get the benefit of the discussion generally, but there is nothing like being in the hot seat to really test yourself.

And *finally*, participating keeps you engaged. Let's face it, not every class is fascinating, and even if it is (or you've convinced yourself it is), your mind may wander, or the professor may be boring. Being ready to participate and actually doing so keeps you engaged so you don't miss anything.

Participating in class may sound scary. And it is scary. But even forgetting about the good reasons discussed above to participate, when you are a lawyer, you will need to become at least somewhat comfortable with public speaking and opening yourself up to criticism no matter what you practice. When you practice law, your arguments will be criticized by your colleagues, the adversary,

10. Being prepared also eases anxiety. Anxiety, at bottom, is about feeling out of control. Being prepared will put you back in control and give you confidence that will help you succeed.

and the court. If you want to litigate, you will also have to get comfortable with speaking in front of the court and juries. Even if you don't litigate, you will likely be put in situations where you have to speak with clients or give presentations. Taking the opportunity to practice in law school is a good, low-stakes way to get some practice and overcome your fears.

B. Notetaking

Staying engaged brings us to the second most important part of class—notetaking. You don't need an extended discussion on the primary purpose of notetaking. You know why you take notes, which is to keep a record of what was said in class. But, again, like many of the tips here, simply taking notes has the added benefit of keeping you engaged and focused. Remember, you will have your computer in front of you. You will check your email. You will look at Facebook, Twitter, or whatever interests you. All of a sudden you will realize that you have been looking at the internet for five minutes and you have missed an important point. And not all important points are obvious. As we discussed, most of the time your knowledge will come from your reading of the cases. You understand them on your own. Of course, some professors will give you black-letter law and you must listen for that. But professors may also give you something more valuable than the black-letter law. You may get their perspective—whether they think the rule or reasoning was sound, whether they think a change in the law is necessary, or even their political leanings. They may guide you into making a connection between cases, finding a legal rule that is not explicit, or a rule they think reconciles seemingly contradictory cases. Sometimes, many times in fact, cases come out in seemingly contradictory outcomes. A professor may have a pet theory on how to reconcile these cases. They may have an explanation. These are alternative rules that you can, and should, use on the exam. As discussed later, an important part of staying ahead of the curve is discussing alternative rules. While many students will struggle to find and apply the right rule, the top students can identify and apply different rules in the same fact pattern. A professor's pet rule, their favored rule, or their wannabe rule, can be the difference between getting a B and an A.

C. After Class

The work is not over. Take five, ten, twenty minutes, whatever you can spare, and review your notes. Read over your notes and find the key points. See the thread between your readings of the day and the discussion in class. Annotate your notes. Reorganize them if necessary. Sometimes the discussion in class takes wild turns and may not lay out the law clearly. If you are working with computer notes (which you should), you can easily move notes around to put the rules together. It's easier to sift through the Socratic nonsense while the information is fresh, rather than later when you go back to create your outline.

III. Scheduling

Scheduling is a fundamental skill for lawyers. Time is a commodity that lawyers sell. The billable hour is at the heart of all legal billing, even when it is not billed by the hour. Even fixed-fee or contingency-fee arrangements consider a lawyer's time. To determine the fixed-fee, a lawyer must determine how much time the project will take. To determine whether to take a case on a contingency, a lawyer must determine how much time the case will take and what the likely outcome will be—if the likely contingency fee exceeds the value of the time, the lawyer should take the case, if not, then it's not worth it.

But proper use of time is not just for lawyers. Entire industries involve teaching people how to use their time. It is, without a doubt, a skill that all successful people have (or pay others to do for them). But there is nothing magical about it. You don't need to read books on it. You simply need to take the time to schedule your time. You already do this for every aspect of your life. You schedule how long you need in the morning to wake up and get ready. You schedule how long it takes to get from place to place. You take into account how long you need to be somewhere and how long it takes to get to the next event. You schedule how long for dinner or a night out. And as a student, you will need to schedule time to study.

When you start law school your schedule will be chosen for you. But that doesn't mean you are not scheduling. What matters is how you divide up the time you have. Lawyers don't get to pick their schedules either. The court, adversaries, and clients dictate when you need to be places and finish things. The best students and lawyers efficiently use the time they are given. As a student, you have a great advantage of knowing exactly what you need to get done during the week. Take advantage of that and plan out your time accordingly. Budget time for reading, case briefing, writing, reviewing, everything you need to do for class. Add in breaks. In the beginning, check the clock as you read. How long does it take you to read a page, ten pages, fifty pages? Get a sense of how long that takes you and use that to budget your reading time. Overestimate to give yourself extra time. Indeed, you should always overestimate so you have extra time in case things come up (which they will).

CHAPTER THREE

Exam Frameworks

If you've been keeping up with your class preparation—reading, briefing, and participating—then you will be ready to prepare for the exam. Preparing for an exam involves outlining and practicing. Once you have your outline, you will use it to practice and, on exam day, you will use the outline during the test. Taking the exam itself involves the active reading techniques we have discussed before, and a simple writing formula we will discuss in this chapter—IRAC.

I. Outlining

A. Create Your Own Outline

Creating your own outline may be the single most important step you take in preparing for the exam. It also may be one of the most daunting. Creating an outline from nothing is hard. It requires that you not only understand the material, but that you arrange it in a way that makes sense to you. That work is important because it requires you to think about the rules you have been learning, how to express them, and how to organize them. That will force you to comprehend the rules (and learn them again, because by this time you will have forgotten them).

Creating your own outline has another important benefit: it creates a mental map of the outline. One way your brain reads and retains information is to perceive blocks of text as physical objects. In fact, your mind creates mental representations of the text that can anchor meaning to structure.[1] This means

1. Jabr, at https://tinyurl.com/TheReadingBrain.

that when you recall information from text, you may actually be remembering *where* in the text it appears rather than the actual substance.[2] That is especially important during exams when the clock is ticking and the stress is high. That ease of navigability reduces cognitive strain, which frees mental resources. In other words, when you have a mental map of the outline, you will have more brain power to focus on the test rather than finding the material. And when you create the outline yourself, you will know the map like the back of your hand.

B. Writing the Outline

So now that you know why you must create your own outline, let's discuss the *how* of creating an outline. It is the most important thing you can do in law school for exam preparation.

First, organization. You need an outline for your outline. But the good news is you already have that starter outline—it is the syllabus. The syllabus is more than just a schedule; it is an outline of the law that your professor created. Professors generally organize their classes in a manner that explains legal rules in an order that makes sense to them. That means the syllabus is the best place to start with your outline. It also functions as a checklist of issues. If it was important enough to be in the syllabus, it is fair game for the exam. So, use that syllabus to organize the topics of your outline.

Second, identify the majority rules within each topic. After your topic heading, break down the rules for each legal theory. You start with the major rule and then break it down into its components. Remember, as discussed in previous chapters, the law is like one of those nesting dolls—you start with big, general legal rules and break them into smaller ones. Often, those broken down parts can be broken down into even smaller parts and so on.

To find the major rules, look at the cases in that chapter. Likely, you have discussed those cases in class, and have identified the major rules that come from those cases. Sometimes, the legal rule is unclear (a favorite of law professors). In that case, there may be a legal rule that arises from a string of cases. If you've been paying attention in class, you will not be surprised when you need to synthesize a rule from a set of cases. Your professors may point out that the rule is unclear or push you into that direction. They might even synthesize the rule for you or have a pet theory on how they think the cases can

---

2. Ernst Z. Rothkopf, *Incidental memory for location of information in text*, Journal of Verbal Learning and Verbal Behavior (1971).

be harmonized. Pay attention, note their theory, and use it. When you take the exam, pointing out that uncertainty and the potential way to synthesize the cases will be beneficial.

Third, include dissents and minority rules in your outline. As will be discussed in the exam writing section below, discussing dissents or minority rules is an easy way to get extra points. Often, your professor will point out the major rule and the minor rule. Sometimes a majority opinion will discuss the minority rule. Other times, you may get a different case discussing a minority rule. Still other times, it will be buried in a dissent. To use these alternative rules, you must, of course, find these rules and put them in your outline. In your outline, directly following a majority rule, or the definition of an element, write out the minority rule. This will allow you to argue in the alternative with those rules in the exam.

Remember, however you choose to organize your outline, or whatever you choose to include, the point of an outline is to help you write your answer to the exam. As discussed below, when you write the exam, you will follow your outline by writing the general rule and then peeling back the layers to set out each subrule before you apply the facts.

As an example of how you put this all together in your outline, consider the rule we discussed in an earlier chapter for common law burglary. In criminal law, you will likely have a section on the syllabus for property crimes. "Property Crimes" would be the topic for this section of the outline. As a subsection, you would have a section for burglary. You then write out the rule statement: "breaking and entering the dwelling of another at night with the intent to commit a felony inside." Then you break that rule down into subrules. You have a section on the elements "breaking," "entering," "dwelling," and so on. Each element of the rule gets its own definition. You find those definitions from the cases you read.

Remember, it is useless to find definitions from materials outside the cases your professor provided (e.g., in hornbooks or commercial outlines). There are countless iterations of legal rules, but the only important ones are those that are in the cases you read or are specifically given to you by your professor. The reason that you must only use those rules is that those are the formulations of the rules that your professor thinks is right, and therefore, those are the right rules to use on the test. If you use an outside source, you may get a differently worded rule, which could drastically change your application.

When finding the rules from the cases, remember that each case you read is generally chosen to discuss one element. For example, there may be a case that discusses the "breaking" element that holds that opening a window satisfies the breaking element. In your outline, you would use that rule to define "breaking" and put a note as to how that case applied the rule. Another case may hold that the "entering" element was satisfied where someone merely placed a body part in an open window. Again, write out that concept in your outline and cite the case in the outline.[3]

Putting that all together, here is an example of a section of an outline for burglary.

Property Crimes

- Burglary
    - Common law Rule
        - Breaking and entering the dwelling of another at night with the intent to commit a felony inside
            - Breaking
                - Creating or enlarging an opening by at least minimal force
                    - Includes—
                        - breaking a window, opening a window, opening a door. *Cite cases with short description of facts.*
                    - Does not include
                        - Climbing through an already open window, or entering with permission. *Cite cases with short description of facts.*
                - Constructive breaking
                    - Entry gained by fraud, threats or intimidation
                    - Example
                        - A person who gets a key to an apartment by saying they will clean the apartment is fraudulent. *Cite case with short description of facts.*

3. Even though you should cite the case in your outline, citing it in your exam is generally not necessary. But paying attention to the facts of those cases, synthesizing them into a general proposition, and writing them in your outline will prepare you for most of the fact patterns you see in your exam. Law school professors are not always creative; they take their cues from cases. The fact-patterns you will see in an exam are almost always some variation on the cases you read.

        - Entry
            - Entry with any part of the body will do, which can be as small as putting a hand into an open window.
        - Dwelling
            - Structure where someone regularly sleeps
        - Of another
            - Cannot burglarize your own house
        - At night
        - Intent to commit a felony inside
            - Specific intent crime
- Modern Statutes
    - Some have eliminated one or more elements of the common law; usually the breaking, at night, or dwelling elements
- NY Burglary (any local jurisdiction you are specifically taught)
    - Third Degree
        - entering or remaining
        - in a building
        - unlawfully
        - with intent to commit any crime (not just felonies)
        - no breaking, dwelling, or nighttime requirements
    - Second Degree
        - add one of the following
            - building is a dwelling
            - non-participant is injured
            - Defendant carries a weapon
    - First Degree
        - Satisfies second degree and
            - defendant knows that he is burglarizing a dwelling
            - plus (one of following)
                - non-participant is injured
                - Defendant carries a weapon

As you can see, an outline provides a road map for your exam. Once you spot an issue involving burglary, you go to that section of your outline and write out all the rules and then plug in the facts. For example, let's take the simple fact pattern of a defendant who enters a home in the afternoon by breaking a window with the intent to steal a television. Your exam answer may proceed as:

> [ISSUE AND RULE STATEMENTS] The issue is whether the defendant committed a burglary. Under common law, a burglary is the breaking and entering the dwelling of another at night with the intent to commit a felony inside. A "breaking" occurs when a person creates or enlarges an opening with minimal force. An "entering" occurs when any part of the body enters the property. A "dwelling" is a structure where someone sleeps.
>
> [APPLY THE FACTS] Here, the defendant broke a window in plaintiff's home intending to steal a television. But, because he entered the home during the day, it does not satisfy the "at night" element, and therefore, is not a common law burglary.
>
> [ALTERNATIVE RULE] Under New York law, however, there is no night-time requirement. To commit a third-degree burglary under New York law, the defendant must unlawfully enter or remain in a building with the intent to commit any crime. If the defendant entered a dwelling, then the crime raises to second-degree. Here, defendant committed second-degree burglary because he broke the window of plaintiff's home with the intent to steal a television.
>
> [HYPOTHETICAL] Finally, the crime could be raised to first-degree if the facts show that the defendant knew he was entering a dwelling and either: (a) injured a non-participant of the crime; or, (b) carried a weapon. Since those facts are absent, however, there was no first-degree crime.

Note the last paragraph. This is the "alternative rule" paragraph discussed earlier where you can earn extra points. If a fact-pattern does not include facts that would allow you to apply a portion of a rule, you can point that out, include the rule, apply it, and get some extra points. Doing that shows your professor that you know all the rules, even though they are not specifically tested. If there are two exams that apply the majority and alternative rules, and one of them discusses some hypothetical facts that would change the outcome, that might get you a bump.[4]

4. Be careful when doing this. You must specifically state in your exam that you are assuming a fact. You do not want to imply that you are misunderstanding the facts in the actual exam.

II. Practicing

Your brain has a capacity (or effort) threshold. It can only do so many things at once, and the less the better. In other words, you can do one thing much better than two. It's not that you can't do two things at one time (you can), it is just that the quality of each task diminishes as you add more tasks. The hardest thing for your mind to do is to keep several ideas at attention at the same time that each require separate actions. It gets harder as you switch tasks, and even harder when you add a time pressure. When this happens, your mind is overloaded and will focus on the most important task at the expense of others.[5]

A law school exam will overload you. It requires you to keep a number of ideas at the front of your mind, while requiring you to do several actions, switching them, and performing them in a time constraint. It requires your brain to read, comprehend, analyze, write, organize, while at the same time requiring you to hold several ideas in your mind—the legal rules, the facts, and how it all fits together. It does all this while requiring you to switch between ideas, topics, tasks—all within a time crunch. This process is not only mentally challenging, it is physically taxing on your mind. Your brain is not meant to perform like this. Instead, your mind, like your body, works on the *law of least effort*, which means that "if there are several ways of achieving the same goal, people eventually gravitate to the least demanding course of action."[6] Indeed, "in the economy of action, effort is a cost, and the acquisition of skill is driven by the balance of benefits and costs."[7] The way to overcome the cost of effort is practice.

By practicing, you can minimize the effort it takes to perform tasks, which will allow you to allocate your energy to the most difficult and important task. Intelligent or talented people excel at difficult tasks because intelligence or talent minimizes the effort it takes to perform multiple tasks; meaning that intelligent people can focus on the most difficult task while automating the more mundane ones. Some people are born with that type of intelligence, but luckily for the rest of us, intelligence is not the only way to minimize effort. Skill can do the same thing as intelligence. And skill is obtained through practice. In that way, practice does not make perfect; it creates skill. Skill helps you

5. Kahneman, at 34–37.
6. Kahneman, at 35.
7. Kahneman at 35.

automate tasks. And automating certain portions of the exam like organization and writing out the general rules means that you can focus on the most important tasks on the test—comprehension and analysis. To make sure you allocate your mind's effort on these activities, you will need to practice to allow yourself to automate tasks.

So, what tasks can you automate for a law school exam? There are at least three: format, rules, and time.

Format. Below, we will discuss the format of answering an exam question. It is fairly simple; issue, rule, application, and conclusion (IRAC). While easy to state, like anything else, the more you practice actually writing in that format, the more that formatting becomes automatic. Instead of thinking how to format, it will come automatically. That will free up your mind's resources.

Rules. In each answer, you will recite a set of legal rules that applies to the question. Just because you know them, or have written them in outline form, does not mean that you are prepared to write them out during the exam. Writing rules into paragraphs after reading an exam prompt is a different exercise for your mind, but it is one you can easily master by taking the time to write a few of them out in practice. For example, try writing the general rules of contract formation into a paragraph. The first time you do it, you will look at your outline and then think about how to organize those rules into paragraph form. It takes effort to do that. Now, do it a second time. You will notice how much faster you did it; how much less effort it took. That saved effort translates directly into more brain power for comprehension and analysis.

Time. You can't change the time pressure, but you can weaken its effect. To do so, take your practice tests under the same time pressure. Not only will you become more skilled at writing through practice, which will free up more time during the test, you will also learn the *feel* of that time. At first, you will have no idea how long it takes you to read a one- or two-page fact pattern, or how much time it will take you to locate the correct rule in your outline, or how long it will take you to write out an answer. By practicing, you will learn how much time it takes for each and you will get better at estimating how much time you need for each task. Eventually that effort will become automated, freeing up your mind for the important tasks and shortening the time it takes to perform them.

If possible, when practicing, you should practice using your professor's old exams if you can find them.[8] The *law of least effort* applies to professors as well.

---

8. Sometimes professors post them online or they are available in exam banks from the school.

This means that professors' exams typically follow a similar format. It's likely that your professor writes a fact pattern for a particular issue over and over again (just with different facts). For example, your contract professor might write a question that hits formation, statute of frauds, and incapacity. That means your answer will follow that pattern as well. You will get skilled at recognizing what rules you need to write out and in what order. All that will be left on exam day is to write these rules out and plug in the facts. You've now automated a few tasks—identifying the rules and writing them out—which frees up resources so that you can incorporate all the facts and spot any unexpected issues the professor adds. If you're lucky, you may be completely prepared for an entire answer on test day. Indeed, on occasion, some professors even reuse the *exact* same tests.[9] If you've encountered that test in your practice runs, then you will be all that much more prepared.

III. The Exam

An exam is an information dump. It is the time for you to show your professor that you know what they taught you. Most exams do not ask you a particular question. They don't ask you what the law is. Most exams present a narrative of facts and ask you to identify the rights, claims, or defenses for each party. Some professors use a matrix that assigns points to certain issues and facts. So, in that way, the more you put in the exam, the more likely you are to get more points. But, of course, you can't just put anything into an exam—it must make sense. And in order for it to make sense, you must be prepared to quickly read the prompt, analyze it, and write a coherent essay.

The key word is "quickly." An exam is not only a test of your comprehension over the semester; it is a performance test under timed, stressful conditions. You don't have the luxury of careful thought. That is why exam preparation is so important. If you've done the work, trust yourself and let the automation do its job.

---

9. While sharply criticized, it happens often. https://abovethelaw.com/2012/01/at-nyu-law-using-the-same-exam-three-times-in-a-row-is-apparently-not-a-problem/; https://abovethelaw.com/2011/12/stop-reusing-your-old-exams-you-lazy-law-school-professors/; https://abovethelaw.com/2016/03/for-the-third-year-in-a-row-professor-reuses-old-contracts-exam/; http://volokh.com/2011/01/18/the-perils-of-reusing-questions-from-past-exams/.

"Quickly" means something else as well: it means that you cannot outline your answer during the exam before you write. If you had all the time in the world, you would read, analyze, outline, and then write. There is no question that outlining is an important step in normal writing. But a law school exam is not a normal writing exercise. Just as the words you choose are resources to explain your answer, the time you use for each step of the exam is a resource you choose. Any time wasted outlining your exam is time wasted on analyzing and writing the exam. You could know all the rules but that will mean nothing if you can't get them onto the paper in time. And if you are following the suggestions in this book, you won't need to outline before writing.

First, while you are actively reading and writing in the margins, you will be doing most of the outline work as you read. You will be identifying issues, facts, and writing those in the margins. So, when it comes time to write, you will have already identified the issues and the pertinent facts in the margins. All you have to do is add the appropriate legal rules and get it on paper. Your active reading techniques become an outline in the margins. Second, reorganizing is a simple task on a computer. Back in the day, I hear people had to hand write exams. But that is not the case anymore. We are lucky enough to be able to write exams on a computer. This means you can write faster, delete things, and move them around. The quicker you start writing, the quicker you can get your thoughts down. If you need to adjust, you can do so—the computer makes that easy. Third, writing reduces stress because it engages your mind. If you are writing, you are not thinking about how stressful the exam is and you are not thinking about time—you are thinking about writing. And finally, as you write, you will identify more issues and facts you need to add to the answer. So, read the prompt, skip the outline, and start writing.

A. Reading the Exam

The first step of taking any exam is to read the entire prompt. And just like everything else you've read, you will be actively reading the exam. If you followed the active reading techniques in Chapter 2 throughout the semester, then they will have become second nature by the time the test arrives. And you will need to use these techniques if you want to skip the outlining (as you should).

Reading an exam involves the same active reading techniques you used in reading your casebook (except the multiple readings because you don't have time). When you read through an exam, read with a pen and annotate the text. This means drawing circles, boxes, brackets, underlines, or stars to mark the different portions of the text—just as you would in your case book. And just as you did during the semester, you should use the same marks for different portions. For example, you may circle issues, underline facts, star important facts, or use whatever marks that make the most sense for you, and preferably, whatever marks you used during the semester. Next, in the margins, you should write Issue 1 or "I-1" or Issue 2 or "I-2" next to the paragraph where an issue first arises. You should also write a quick note as to what type of issue, for example "I-1, formation," or "I-2, statute of frauds." Then, as you underline facts in the text, you can write a note in the margin linking that fact to an issue.

You should assume that all the facts in an exam prompt are relevant. Remember that exam prompts must be economical. Professors know that they can include only so much information so that you have time to write an answer. And that means they must cram in as much information into as short of an exam prompt as possible. Because of that, every sentence in the exam prompt is likely important. Every sentence likely has some relevance and meaning. Although professors will warn you to disregard irrelevant facts in the exam, they hardly ever include any in the actual exam. They just don't. They are not trying to trick you. There is enough information that they need to provide so you can answer the question and for them to be able to distinguish your paper from another. There simply isn't room for wasted facts. But even if they do give you irrelevant facts, you will know. They will stand out. Spending time looking for irrelevant facts is wasted time. Your default should be that every fact has some relevance and should be included somewhere in your answer.

Assuming every fact is important provides an added benefit; it provides you with a checklist to make sure you are hitting all the relevant issues. If you have not incorporated a fact, then you are almost certainly missing something. Each fact is a key piece of information the professor added to alert you to an issue or to include in your analysis. If you have not included a fact in the exam prompt, think hard about whether adding or omitting this fact affects your answer. Think hard about whether this fact raises an issue you have not addressed. If you're certain it does not add anything, then you can be confident that you didn't miss something. More times than not, however, when you find a fact you have not incorporated, you will realize you missed something. Then you just add the fact and score some more points.

B. Writing the Exam—IRAC

Once you've read the exam and marked it up, you are ready to write. The organization technique for writing is the same as any argument. It is a syllogism. As discussed in Chapter 1, a syllogism consists of a major premise (the legal rule), a minor premise (the application of facts), and the conclusion. Add an issue statement up front (the question you are answering), and you get the familiar format of IRAC; Issue, Rule, Application, and Conclusion.

IRAC is the preferred form for law school exams (and legal writing) because it follows the basic syllogistic form that all good legal arguments follow. But IRAC has another advantage over other potential formats because of the fluency-effect. The *fluency-effect* relates to the way a person processes information subconsciously. It means that "if the form of the information is difficult to assimilate, that affects our judgments about the substance of that information."[10] But if the information is simple to read and follows a familiar format, a person forms a more favorable position about it, without regard to the substance. For lawyers, that form is IRAC because it is a form that all lawyers are taught and constantly read in cases. And if they didn't learn it in school, they certainly learned it for the bar exam. The bar examiners expect to read essays in IRAC form. Law professors, too, were taught the IRAC form. Additionally, good judges write in IRAC form. You will notice as you read cases, that the easiest ones to digest are those in IRAC form. The judge identifies the issue, discusses what rule should apply, applies it, and reaches a conclusion. As such, your professors will expect to see that form in your writing because that is the form they are familiar reading. It is unconscious and affects their assessment of the substance without them knowing it. When they see a different format, it is harder for them to understand, even if the substance is the same. So following IRAC is not only an easy format to follow, it allows you to take advantage of the fluency effect, and disregarding it may work against you.

1. Issue

Before you do anything, you must spot the issue. It is the most important thing you can do on an exam because, of course, it sets the stage for your answer. The one thing that law school exams are notorious for are failing to identify the question—law school exams don't ask you to answer a direct question. Instead, exams present you with a narration of facts, and at the end, prompt you with something broad like, "discuss the issues," or "discuss the parties' claims and defenses." Now, although this book cannot teach you how to spot particular issues on a particular exam, the process you have engaged in up to this point will prepare you to spot those issues quicker than others. Proper reading, class participation, and outlining will prepare you. It is all part of the automation process that will free up your resources to focus on the exam.

---

10. Mlodinow, at 22.

Once you've spotted the issue, the format is: The [first] issue is whether [fill in with the question you are about to answer]. That is your issue statement. It is your topic sentence. The explanation of what rules you will be applying will come right after that.

For example, your first issue in a constitutional law exam may be related to standing (i.e., whether the plaintiff is a proper party to bring the case). Thus, your issue statement would be no more complicated than, "The first issue is whether the plaintiff has standing." Then you would set out the rules that apply to standing. In a contracts exam, it might be, "The issue is whether X and Y entered into an enforceable contract." Then set out the rules that determine whether an enforceable contract existed. Simple as that.[11]

If you are having trouble spotting the issue, remember that you have a checklist of potential issues from the syllabus and your outline. The major issues you see in an exam will likely follow your syllabus and outline. Let's take contracts for example. The first major subject you learn will likely be contract formation; i.e., what constitutes an enforceable contract. The next major subject you may learn is defenses. And finally, damages. In between all those major topics will be all the various rules and subrules of each. If you are having trouble spotting an issue, just take a look at your syllabus and outline and see what issues are available. Most likely, this will trigger you to see that issue in the exam.

Also, as we discussed before, your professor has created that syllabus in a manner they believe is most logical. Thus, you might find that issues arise in an exam in the same order as they appear on the exam. And you should be prepared to discuss them in that order.

---

11. Note that this simple form for issue statements is meant only for exams. When you are writing in your legal writing class, for example, your issue statement will not be so simple. In your legal writing class, you should weave in facts and be more specific about the issue (e.g., the issue is whether X and Y had a meeting of the minds [more specific element of enforceable contracts] where they did [weave in facts]). Of course, there is nothing stopping you from creating issue statements on an exam like you would do in a paper course; but you do not need to. Remember, the most important aspects of an exam are speed and points. The quicker you identify the issue, the quicker you can move on to identifying the rules and applying them. So, while you may get some style points by having a more sophisticated issue statement, it is simply a waste of time because you will be identifying those rules and facts in the following sentences. Where speed and quantity is king, the simple issue statement is sufficient. The time in crafting an elegant issue statement on an exam is wasted time.

2. Rule

Once you've written the issue, write the legal rule that answers that question. This is the major premise of the syllogism that we discussed back in Chapter 1. Start broadly with the main rule that identifies each element and then peel back the layers of each element or factor. You could even mix in a policy explanation of the doctrine if it makes sense and you have time.

For example, take standing. After you write that the issue is whether the plaintiff has standing, you write out the elements of standing, which are: "To establish standing a plaintiff must show: (1) injury in fact, (2) causation, and (3) redressability." You could also state a bit of background on the policy reason for standing if you'd like and have the time.

In subsequent paragraphs, you will open by identifying the element you will analyze in that paragraph. For example, after your opening paragraph, you would repeat that "the first element of standing is injury in fact." You then break that broad rule statement down by explaining what it means and what it takes to satisfy the rule: "An injury in fact requires a plaintiff to show an actual and concrete injury." You would then define the contours of "actual and concrete injury" by stating what types of injuries satisfy the rule, or what types of injuries have been found that do *not* satisfy the rule. The latter is more likely to earn you points and show the professor you've been listening. By stating what does not satisfy the rule, you will be incorporating the facts of the cases. For example, you may read a case stating that stigmatic injuries do not satisfy the rule. Even if there is no stigmatic injury presented in the fact pattern, by identifying this rule, you are defining the contours of the rule and showing the professor you've been paying attention. Again, that rule about stigmatic injury will be in your outline, so it is easy to just write them out as you work through your outline.

Because you know the rule portion will not change, you can prepare for certain rules you expect to be tested on by actually writing out paragraphs of rule statements during practice. It is simple for you to practice writing out the rule portions. You may think that such an exercise is wasteful, but it is not. Remember that this type of practice reduces your cognitive strain during the exam because instead of taking that effort to think how to express the rules, you've already done that and thus freed up your brain to do the hard thinking. For example, if you know you are going to get a standing question on an exam, you can practice writing out a paragraph of the rule statement and its subrules and even its policy. You could conceivably do this with every issue in your outline. It can be a great way to practice, reduce cognitive strain, and save time in the exam.

3. Application

Once you've identified the issue and written out the rules, you apply the facts to the rules. What you should do is devote a paragraph to each element of the rule and then apply the relevant facts to that portion of the rule. Practically, this means that you repeat the element you are discussing at the top of the paragraph and then add the facts that establish or rebut that element.

Following our standing example, once you set out the broad rules in your opening paragraph, and then the subrules in another, you simply apply the facts that relate to those rules. When you are ready to apply the facts, indicate you are doing so with a logical connector like, "here" or "in this case," and then apply the facts. To apply the facts, you just plug in the facts to the rule statements. So following our standing example, if you wrote the rule that "an injury in fact requires a plaintiff to show an actual and concrete injury," then your application would explain why or why there is not an actual and concrete injury. For example, "the plaintiff does [or does not] have an injury-in-fact because it suffered [list injuries or explain the lack of injury]."

Generally, you do not need to discuss the facts of cases you read in class. In your paper course and in actual legal writing, you would discuss the facts of an analogous case and then show how your facts are just like those (if you like the result of that case) or nothing like those (if you don't like the result of that case). But, in an exam, there is no need to discuss the facts of cases you have read. It would take too long and it is something you cannot adequately prepare for. It is more than sufficient to state the rule, explain it, and then plug in the facts that relate to that rule.

4. Conclusion

There is no magic in the conclusion. In each paragraph you should make a conclusion as to that paragraph. As discussed above in the rule section, your first paragraph will state all the elements the plaintiff must satisfy for that issue. To end that paragraph, you can include a broad conclusion for every element. You can state it as quickly as, "the plaintiff will be able to establish these elements," or more detailed by adding some facts such as, "the plaintiff will be able to establish these elements because: (1) she was injured from X; (2) that injury was caused by defendants doing Y; and (3) the court can redress the problem by doing Z."

For each subsequent paragraph where you discuss a different element, you conclude on that element. For those conclusions you stick to the element and the facts for that element. And so on, until you've gone through all the elements. After you have discussed all the elements, you then conclude as to the entire issue. So, even though you have stated your conclusion up front in the opening paragraph, and then conclusions for each element in subsequent paragraphs, you must state it again and answer your issue statement. It can be as simple as restating your issue as a conclusion. Following our example on standing, you might state "Therefore, the plaintiff has established standing." You then move on to your next issue.

5. The What-If Paragraph

What if the rules or facts were different? You'd likely get a different outcome, right? Engaging in that analysis is an opportunity to differentiate yourself and show your professor you have been paying attention. You can do this in two ways: by applying an alternative rule or a hypothetical fact.

Generally, law professors teach you alternative rules. That minority rule may come from a minority of states or it might come from a dissent. But wherever it comes from, remember that your professor taught you those rules for a reason. Usually, it is because the application of that alternative rule will affect the outcome of a given fact pattern. So, don't waste that knowledge. If you have time, use that different rule to set up a paragraph at the end of your exam. Say something like, "Under the minority rule...." And then plug the facts into that rule. You've now added an entire extra paragraph of rules and analysis that can get you more points.

You can do the same thing with the facts. What if the plaintiff did X instead of Y? Sometimes, by assuming different facts (once you've applied the actual facts), you may be able to apply some subrule that you were unable to discuss in the core analysis. Sometimes, rules only apply when particular facts are present. If the facts don't trigger that rule, then you would never get to discuss that exception or subrule. But if you assume the facts went that way, then you get to apply that rule and show the professor how much you know. Just make sure you first apply the facts *as they are written* and then expressly state that you are assuming a different fact so that it is clear you understand the facts that were written.

6. Indicator Words

Finally, it is important to use discourse markers, indicator words, and transition words throughout your writing. Discourse markers are words or phrases that organize writing and send a signal to the reader as to what *section* of the argument they are reading. Indicator words help to show what *part* of the argument is a premise or conclusion. Transition words show that you are moving from discussing one issue to another.

Start paragraphs with appropriate transition words and guideposts. So, you may start each paragraph with *First*, *Second*, *Third*, and *Finally*. For example, *First,* the plaintiff must show an injury in fact, or "the first element is X." Then you start the next paragraph with, "*Second,* the plaintiff must show Y," or "next, the plaintiff must show Y." This is especially important with conclusions, and again, there is nothing special here. Use a term like "thus," "therefore," "consequently," "accordingly," or "it follows that," to indicate that you are concluding.

There is no need to be fancy with your writing and indicator words, but just like all other writing, these markers are important to use to guide your reader. Again, this may sound simple and boring, but you're not trying to wow the reader with your literary skills here; you are trying to provide knowledge in a manner they can quickly process. Remember the fluency effect as well, using these types of markers will trigger positive assumptions about your writing and make it more likely for your professor to understand your writing easily. Similarly, using logical connectives plays a heuristic[12] role for your reader that actually exaggerates the degree of logical dependence, thus influencing your reader to accept the argument.[13]

12. A "heuristic" is a rule of thumb your mind uses to quickly analyze information. Thaler, at 45. Thus, the use of logical connectors triggers your reader's mind to accept relationships at first glance.

13. Hugo Mercier & Dan Sperber, *The Enigma of Reason*, at 166 (2017).

CHAPTER FOUR

Frameworks for Paper Courses

A *paper course* is a class that you write a paper for rather than sit for an exam. People think paper courses are less work or easier than exam courses. Not true. Paper courses require just as much effort, if not more, than exam courses. For one, you will have just as much reading, note taking, and reviewing as you would in any other class. Second, the research and writing required to produce a paper may actually take *more* time and effort than studying for and taking an exam. With an exam, you create an outline and practice. With a paper, you have research, outlining, writing, and then more writing. It is that "more writing" part that will distinguish you, because, at bottom, great writing is rewriting. And that takes time. Third, there is no room for typos, blue-booking errors, or poor organization. In an exam, those errors may be forgiven as a result of the time crunch. But, when you write a paper, it must be error free. When a course ends in a paper, both the little and big things matter.

That is not meant to discourage you from taking paper courses. To the contrary, you should seek out paper courses. Lawyers are professional writers. And writing is the one thing that you can really practice at law school. Paper courses provide that necessary practice. But regardless of whether you seek them out, there are paper courses you will have to take—most notably, the one in your first-year writing course. The following provides a framework for your paper courses.

I. Follow the Rules

The most important rule is to follow your professor's rules. Despite what you may think about writing, your legal writing course is the least creative course in law school. After learning the basics of legal research, your principal task in this class will be to produce papers. It might be a memorandum, a trial brief, or an appellate brief. The point of this class is not to dazzle your professor with your legal or creative genius—the point is to show your professor that you can follow the rules and produce a paper that includes all the bells and whistles.

That means, first and foremost, following the formatting rules. Your professor will likely provide you with rules as to typeface, font size, spacing, headings, subheadings, indentation, page limitations, etc. Follow every single instruction, read them over, and read them again. Use your professor's instructions to write yourself a checklist. You can then use that before you hand in the paper. Every single rule you get right is another point—an easy point.

Indeed, hyper-sensitivity to formatting is actually preparing you to practice law. Courts around the country have detailed instructions on almost every aspect of formatting briefs. If your brief does not conform to these formatting requirements, your brief could be rejected. Sometimes you can fix the error and refile; other times, you could be subject to sanctions or your brief could even be stricken, leaving your side without an argument. In other words, formatting is important.

Your legal writing professor will teach you how to substantively format your paper. Unless your professor tells you otherwise, it will be IRAC. Your legal writing professor will walk you through how to write each section. Your professor may have a way they like to format the issue statement—follow it. Your professor may tell you how to write the rule paragraph—follow it. You will get instructions on how to apply the law to the facts and write the conclusion—follow every single instruction. Where you don't have sufficient instruction, ask a student that has been through that class or the teaching assistant, if there is one. Again, the number one rule is to follow *your* professor's rules.

Another important aspect of your first-year writing course is learning and mastering The Bluebook. The Bluebook is your guide for legal citation. The Bluebook contains rules on how to cite cases, statutes, online sources, law reviews, and record cites. You will likely be graded on whether your citations conform to The Bluebook. So, that is another easy way to gain (or lose) points. The more you master it, the better off you will be. The skills you use in following The Bluebook will follow you all through law school and beyond.

While reading a rulebook may be some of the driest and most boring material you will read, you must read the entire thing. To do that, I would not suggest reading it like a novel. When you first start your legal writing class, take 20 minutes a day, or less, and read a chapter. That will get you familiar with what is in The Bluebook and where it can be found. There is no need to memorize it, but reading it through will provide you with a familiarity that will aid you in law school and beyond.

II. Style

Follow the major rulebooks on style and grammar. Get very comfortable with consulting them for everything from when to use capitals to the proper use of commas and semicolons. Your school's law review likely has a style manual they follow. Get it and use that. While The Bluebook will be your primary style book, it does not contain all the rules you need. For example, The Bluebook does not cover the proper use of semicolons, or the difference between a hyphen, an en-dash, and an em-dash, or explains the parts of grammar. For all that, you need a book on style. If you don't know the rulebook your law review prefers, use The Chicago Manual of Style or The Redbook by Bryan Garner.[1]

We have all heard the word "style" with reference to writing. Usually, people are using that word to refer to some sort of individual style, and people think they need to use big words or complicated sentences to differentiate themselves. Forget that. The only style you have for legal writing is bland. Use plain language all the time. Never use a word you have to look up or think someone else might have to. Strip your paper of extra words, adjectives, and adverbs. Write in the active voice, which means that your sentences follow this format: subject-action-object. In other words, John kicked the ball. Not, the ball was kicked by John (passive).[2]

---

1. Other great books that cover the basics on writing are The Elements of Style by Strunk and White and Plain English for Lawyers by Richard C. Wydick.

2. There is a place for the passive voice. You should use the passive voice when you are attempting to downplay a certain fact. Thus, a prosecutor may say that John stole the ball, but John's defense counsel may state that the ball was taken by John. You can also use the passive voice for variety to break up your flow. Your focus should never be to create variety, but it does have its place and you will know when it is needed as you proof your work.

You have one goal when writing—to inform your audience. You inform your audience of the facts, the legal rules, the relevant cases, and, most importantly for lawyers, why you're right. Assume your audience knows nothing and has little time to understand. Explain it to them in the simplest language possible and as quickly as possible. Remember, your audience consists of busy people with little time and even less patience. You must be direct and to the point. Their attention is something they are willing to give to you, but eager to take back. So never lose sight of that precious little attention they give you, and never make them struggle to understand. A reader should know everything they need to know from your paper quickly.

It is difficult to write concisely and include everything you want. It's long-been said that: "If I had more time, I would have written a shorter letter."[3] It is fairly easy to go on and on, but it is difficult to say it concisely. Unlike college papers, you may find yourself surprised when you get a 5-, 10-, or 15-page limit, and you struggle to stay *within* the page limits rather than fill them up.

All of that takes time. A lot of time. You don't just put pen to paper when writing. It takes preparation and planning. It takes writing and rewriting, and rewriting and more rewriting. Earnest Hemingway once said that "the only kind of writing is rewriting." No one ever submits a first draft. Nor should you. Good writing takes time. And there is no such thing as good legal writing; there is only good writing.

Finally, make sure to schedule enough time for each step of the writing process. Then schedule more. In fact, whatever time you think you need, double it. Schedule some time away from your writing as well. Walking away from your writing will allow you to look at it with fresh eyes when you return.

III. Outlining

Unlike writing an exam, writing papers *requires* outlining. It is a mistake to think that skipping the outline will save you time. As Justice Scalia said, "eliminating this step is a false economy."[4] If you properly outline, the paper will write itself; skip it and it will take you twice as long to produce a well-written product (if you ever get there).

---

3. This quote has been attributed to Mark Twain, George Bernard Shaw, Voltaire, Blaise Pascal, Johann Wolfgang von Goethe, Winston Churchill, Pliny the Younger, Cato, Cicero, Bill Clinton, and Benjamin Franklin. https://quoteinvestigator.com/2012/04/28/shorter-letter/.

4. Scalia & Garner, at 70.

Remember that, even before outlining, the first step is to carefully read the materials you are given. Use all the reading techniques we discussed in Chapter 2. Once you understand the case, identify the issues you need to research. While researching, outline as you research—plug the cases you find into the sections of the brief. It's ok for it to be messy at first. It will surely change as you keep researching and refining your analysis, but that is simple while using a computer—just drag or copy them into the right place.

The format of your outline will eventually look like everything else you write—IRAC. Here is a form for an outline:

Paper Outline

I. Issue 1
  a. Thesis statement
    i. In a brief, this will be a statement of what you want the court to do: The court should [deny/grant] the motion because X.[5]
  b. Rule
    i. Quote cases setting forth the rule statement.
  c. Element 1
    i. Case statements explaining element 1
    ii. Favorable cases
    iii. Unfavorable cases
      1. Distinguish
  d. Element 2
    i. Case statements explaining element 2
    ii. Favorable cases
    iii. Unfavorable cases
      1. Distinguish
  e. Conclusion

5. Don't tell the Court what it "must" do. That language is too strong when writing to the Court. You may very well think the Court "must" agree with you, but it doesn't have to. So use the word "should" instead.

This format is merely a guideline you might use while researching to organize your cases. As you move toward writing, your outline may change. You may find that element 2 goes before element 1, or that you don't need to discuss element 1 in the same detail as element 2. Eventually, your outline will change from mere organization to a fully formed outline. Once you have that all down, the writing will come naturally.

IV. Writing

A. Issue

In Chapter 3, we discussed writing issue statements for an exam. For purposes of an exam, where speed is key, the issue statement is simple; it merely identifies the broad legal issue you are answering. For example, the [first] issue is whether [fill in with the question you are about to answer]. With papers, however, your issue statements must combine facts and law. So instead of simply asking the question of what broad legal rule must be answered, you will need to add more precise rules and facts to that issue statement. For example, instead of "whether there is standing," you could say, "whether Plaintiff suffered an actual and concrete injury traceable to [this is a more precise definition of standing] Defendant's acts of X, Y, and Z [facts]." The first part substitutes the broad legal question, whether there is standing, for the more precise formulation of the legal rules.

Or you could use the deep-issue statement advocated by Justice Scalia and Bryan Garner. The deep-issue statement is basically a syllogism that produces your answer. It is about three sentences, no longer than 75 words, in the form premise-premise-question. The premises are the rule and a fact about your case.[6] For example: "To plead fraud, a plaintiff must plead, among others, a misrepresentation of present fact, and not a future one. The Plaintiff pleaded that Defendant lied to her about the number of widgets he could produce. Did the Plaintiff plead a misrepresentation of fact?" The deep-issue statement basically answers itself. It gives enough for anyone picking up the memo to understand the issue immediately

But as always, use the form your professor advises. Do not use other forms if they violate the first rule, which is to follow your professor's rules. If your professor provides you with a different format for writing issue statements—use it.

---

6. *See* Scalia & Garner, at 85–88.

B. Rule Statement

When writing a paper, the first thing you need are cases stating the rule. Depending on the issue, you could find hundreds or thousands of cases, but you really only need one.

So, how do you pick which case to use? There are three things to consider. *First*, you need a case that you can quote the rule word for word. When you are writing the rule statement, you *do not* want to put it into your own words. Words matter. Every single word you add or change has an effect on the rule and its application. So, don't go changing words in your rule statement. Find a case that you can quote the rule and its elements, full stop. *Second*, try to find a case from the highest court in your jurisdiction. *Third*, use a case you are going to discuss in detail that applies to your facts. Again, you may find many cases that lay out the rule very clearly. But there is no need to pick a random case to use as your rule. If you can find a case you are going to discuss that has a clear rule statement, use that one.

Those considerations for choosing a case as the rule statement are all you need when writing an objective memorandum. When you are writing a persuasive paper, such as a brief, however, there is another consideration—does the case go your way? For example, if you are writing a brief on behalf of a defendant charged with burglary, you will have many cases to choose from that cite the rule—even ones, perhaps, from the highest court in your jurisdiction. All things being equal, though, you want to choose a binding case that goes your way (a case where the party won, or lost, depending on your position).

Of course, you may not ignore negative, relevant authority. Not only is it unethical,[7] but your opponent will no doubt raise those cases, and it is imperative that you address them. But that doesn't mean they are your leading cases. Instead, lead with your positive argument, and then distinguish those negative cases.

C. Application

Once you've identified your rule statement, the next step is to apply the rule. Applying the rule starts with breaking down the rule into elements. Then you devote a paragraph to discuss each element. So, following your rule statement,

---

7. ABA Model Rules 3.3(a)(2) ("A lawyer shall not knowingly: ... fail to disclose to the tribunal legal authority in the controlling jurisdiction known to the lawyer to be directly adverse to the position of the client and not disclosed by opposing counsel.").

in an objective memo, your next paragraph will start with a thesis statement that simply states the element. That might be: "the first element the party must satisfy is [element]." If it is an advocacy memo, you combine the element with your conclusion. You may say, "the party [has/has not] satisfied the [first element] because [reasons]."

In the following paragraphs, you discuss and apply the cases. When discussing cases, you do not discuss them one by one and then apply your facts to each case, one by one. What you want to do is to explain each case together, and then apply to your facts. Remember, what you are doing when discussing and applying cases is analogical reasoning. As discussed in Chapter 2, analogies are strong or weak depending on how many relevant qualities each part of the analogy shares. With cases, the relevant qualities are the facts. Thus, if case 1 has facts a, b, c, and d, and your case shares facts a, b, and c, then the analogy is strong. If your case shares only fact a, then that analogy is weak. What you do when you discuss multiple cases is basically set out the facts of each case and then analogize. So, you may state that case 1 has facts a, b, c, and d, and went way x. Then, case 2 has facts a, b, c, d, and e, and also went way x. Then you apply both to your case and conclude that your case should come out the same way.

You do the same thing for distinguishing cases that don't go your way. Put them all together and sweep them away together. With distinguishing cases, the best thing you can do is find a common theme among the cases. In other words, negative cases 1 and 2 both share fact x, and, in contrast here, this case does not have fact x.[8]

D. Conclusion

The conclusion remains simple. It answers your issue or tells the court what you want it to do. Use a transition word like, "thus," "therefore", "in sum [or, in short]", and state your conclusion. For example, "thus, party A has established [the elements or broad rule]," or "therefore, the court should grant/deny party A's motion because party A has established all the elements of its claim."

---

8. Again, use a simple transition word to show that you have moved on from discussing those cases to applying them to your case. A few simple ones include, "in contrast here," "but here," "unlike X and Y, here." You should avoid *however* in starting a transition sentence. While you may use *however* to start a sentence in certain instances, most writing authorities instruct that *however* comes in the middle of a sentence. Thus, the way to transition with *however* would be: "in this case, however, X."

V. Oral Argument

Your first-year writing course may also include a mock oral argument. If it does, it will likely be arguing the motion or appeal you briefed. The good news about oral argument is that you've already done just about all of the hard work. All the information you need for oral argument is in the background material, your paper, your opponent's paper, and, of course, the cases. That's it. Oral argument is a self-contained exercise. You don't have to do further research. All you need to do is know the information and be prepared to say it. That doesn't mean that you memorize everything. You can't. And you shouldn't put that type of pressure on yourself. Oral argument is no different than any other activity we have discussed. Once you do the necessary preparation—you must trust yourself.

So, let's talk about that preparation. The point of this preparation is to know the information like the back of your hand. Once you've gathered all your information, print it out so you can read it front to back. Read your paper again; read your opponent's paper again; and read all the cases again. Use all the active reading techniques we discussed in Chapter 2, including marking up the documents. As you'll recall, writing on text aids comprehension and creates mental maps. When you are in oral argument, you won't have time to read the materials while arguing to find a specific point. That is why creating a mental map of the page is imperative for your recall. And if you are asked for a quote, or need to look at the materials to recall something, creating a physical map of the text with your markings will enable you to find the information you are seeking quickly. Instead of searching for just a word in all your pages, you now have the added benefit of using the landmarks you created to aid your search. All the markings you make in your text—underlines, circles, asterisks—all help to differentiate different sections of text, and thus, help you to differentiate and find the text you need quickly.

Now that you have your marked-up documents, prepare to *not* rely on them. Oral argument is a conversation. You are not there to read a speech, and you are certainly not there to recite your brief. You are there to present your argument and answer questions. You are there to establish trust by showing that you know what you are talking about. That means you know the facts, the issues, the law, and how it all fits together. That also means you know what you don't know. You must concede points when necessary but be prepared to pivot right back to your strong points and explain why those points outweigh your concession. To be prepared to do this, you need to create an outline of your major points and best supporting evidence and rebuttals for each. You should also have a short outline of the major cases, including key facts and holdings.

Your outline for the oral argument should be no more than two pages. You should place two sheets of paper next to each other in a folder, a binder, or just place them on the podium. But it is important that these two pages sit next to each other and that you do not need to flip through paper to find the information you need. While you will always have your backup documents for emergencies (and peace of mind), the truth is, you will not have time to consult a three-inch binder during oral argument. Oral argument typically lasts no more than 15 minutes. That may sound like a long time, especially if you are nervous. But it is not. You will be through your argument before you know it. And then you will think of all the things you wish you had said, but didn't (which is completely normal).

Although you should not memorize or read while arguing, many lawyers have a script for a one sentence opening: *May it please the Court, my name is _____, I represent ______, and the Court should do X because Y.* X is your conclusion; the court should grant/deny the motion, or affirm/reverse the judgment. The Y are your reasons, and you can use your major point headings to guide you. This gives you some grounding when you get up there and it gives the court a roadmap for your argument. You then start with the issue you want to discuss. You should not start with a recitation of the facts. Assume the judges or your professors know the facts. That doesn't mean you ignore them, of course; instead, weave them into your argument where appropriate. But again, consult the first rule: if your professor advises you to recount the facts, do it.

Here is a guideline for the two-page outline.

May it please the Court, my name is ___, and I represent ____, and the Court should do X because Y. I. Point Heading One A. Standard Quote the standard B. Apply the facts Fact 1 Fact 2 C. Rebuttal Identify your opponent's argument and why it is wrong II. Point Heading Two A. Standard Quote the standard B. Apply the facts Fact 1 Fact 2 C. Rebuttal Identify your opponent's argument and why it is wrong	**Cases** 1. A v. B Relevant Facts Holding Similarity/Distinguish 2. C v. D Relevant Facts Holding Similarity/Distinguish

Now, again, this is just a guideline. Sometimes you may need more or less. Sometimes, you'll need a separate page or pages for your case summaries. You may want to organize it totally differently. That is fine. The point is, whatever you do, you need to do it in a way that makes you nimble. And to be nimble, you need to practice with your materials. You need to practice standing with your materials, speaking the words, and moving the pages if you need to. All this will make you faster and more articulate during oral argument.

When you practice, be ready to speak your entire argument without questions. Having a cold bench (one that doesn't ask any questions) is highly unusual, and much harder in some ways than having a hot bench (which asks many questions), but you must be prepared for it. When you practice, get up, put your pages in front of you, and speak your argument out loud. State your opening and then state each argument out loud. Once you've stated your opening, you start with your first issue. You give your main point heading argument, and then you articulate the standard and why the facts go your way. You then state your opponent's argument and explain why it's wrong. You then move on to issue two. And so on, until you conclude.

While you should be prepared to speak without questions, that is highly unlikely. The more likely scenario is that you will be peppered with questions within a minute of you speaking. That means you should anticipate questions and have answers ready. To do that, think about questions you might ask of yourself. Think about the other side's arguments and what questions the judge may ask you about their argument. Focus on their best cases and their best arguments and picture a judge asking you why they are wrong and you are right.

You must stand and practice speaking aloud because it will feel different than writing or saying the arguments in your head. You must feel yourself standing up, feel the words in your mouth, and hear those words spoken. You will find that you become sharper, more succinct, and more articulate each time you practice. This will translate into a better performance during oral argument. And while you may think you cannot anticipate all the questions you will get, you may find that your practice of speaking the words out loud will trigger questions within you that you can prepare answering.

Your final practices should be an actual moot (practice) in front of someone else. Ideally, this will be with fellow students who have had time to read the briefs. But you can also practice in front of someone who hasn't read the case. It is also worthwhile to practice in front of someone who is not a lawyer or law student. Presenting your argument to someone who is not a lawyer is a beneficial technique because it helps you explain your case to anyone and a nonlawyer likely will raise issues that you may not have thought of. They may ask questions that you don't know, or that you didn't think were relevant. That is invaluable. You may find that you were wrong in ignoring that piece of information, that you missed a key fact for understanding, or maybe that fact provides context that a normal person may want to hear.

Bottom line, practice does not make perfect, but it makes you prepared. When you are prepared, you can trust yourself to get up there and handle whatever comes. And you will.

CHAPTER FIVE

Frameworks for Law Review and Moot Court

After grades, there are two other important marks to hit: law review and moot court. Both are important because employers will expect to see them on your resume. But they are more than empty markers; each has practical value and are proxies for skills that you can offer an employer out of law school. In law review, you will learn and practice the basics of The Bluebook, grammar, and proofing another's work (over and over). That is a critical skill you will need as a junior attorney. Whether your first job is a clerkship, government, a firm, or in-house, your ability to proof another's work will be a critical skill. Law review will give you that skill, and it will also improve your own work. In moot court, you will get a chance to hone and practice your oral advocacy skills. Being a strong oral advocate is a matter of practice, and moot court gives you that opportunity. As a result, taking these activities seriously is important to your success in law school, which, ultimately, is to succeed out of law school.

I. Law Review

Law review is a student run scholarly journal focusing on legal issues. Each school has many different law reviews that focus on different legal issues. But each school also has a flagship law review, that is the school's main law review and focuses on general issues. Making the flagship law review is another key marker in your success.

To make law review requires all the skills previously discussed in this book. It first requires that you get good grades, which you will already have. Following that, making law review follows the same pattern as writing a paper in your paper courses. And like paper courses, the most important rule is to read the rules. Each law review will have its own rules, processes, and requirements. You must read those rules and follow them. Luckily, you don't need to know all those rules (and I don't need to discuss them) because all you need to do is follow the frameworks for writing discussed in Chapter 4. If all your law review requires is a threshold grade point average, then you have that down already.

There may also be a "write-on." A "write-on" is the portion of your application where you submit a paper on a topic of the law review's choosing—generally a recent Supreme Court decision. You are thus *writing* to get *on* law review—a "write-on." Whatever you call it, it is just another paper. You will use the same skills you learned in your writing class: closely reading the directions, reviewing the materials provided, researching if necessary, and writing an error-free document. Simple as that. Remember, you may not think so, but executing the small things perfectly will put you heads and shoulders above your classmates.

Law review also provides you with an opportunity to practice skills that you will use in the real world—proofing another's work and writing. Proofing another's work is a key skill for your early practice and law review may be one of the only places in law school where you will learn and practice that skill. In your classes, you are learning the law and, yes, being critical of what you read. But, in class, you are not reading the cases with an eye towards whether the grammar or citation form is right. Your ability to review another's work, however, will be critical when you start practicing law. Indeed, many times, your employers, whoever they are, judges, lawyers, businesses, will depend on you to check their writing. And lawyers and judges will expect perfection in their written product and will count on you to make sure it is.[1]

In order to be good at checking another's work, you must learn and use fundamental grammar and cite checking skills. Law review teaches you those skills through practice. On law review, you will be reading and proofing the law review

1. You should strive for the same in your writing as a law student (and beyond). While perfection in and for itself is not admirable, the point of perfection in writing has an independent importance. When you are trying to persuade a judge, or even another party, that you are right, little things like improper grammar or typos can put them off. It is important not only to be right, but for the reader to want you to be right. And, as a lawyer, almost no one you write for is rooting for you to be right or has an interest in you being right. So you have to be extra vigilant in your writing. And if you happen to get a reader who is put off by improper grammar or typos, then you are in trouble. While most people, including lawyers and judges, will forgive those mistakes, you have to write for the person who won't forgive you because you never know when that person will be your reader.

articles that are published in your law review. To do that proofing, you will need to consult grammar guides and The Bluebook regularly. That work will get you comfortable with the rules and they will become second-nature to you, or at the very least will teach you where to look. That experience is invaluable. Not only will you learn a real-life skill that you will immediately apply in law jobs, but it will translate into your own writing. By identifying and correcting the mistakes of others, you will be less likely to commit them yourself.

Law review also gives you another opportunity for writing—writing your own law review article, which has a chance to get published with the law review. After you've sharpened your skills checking another's work during your first year of law review, you will get to apply those skills to writing a note. A note is a journal article written by a law student that can be published by that school's law review. The note is your opportunity to choose a topic you are interested in, research it, and write on it. The benefits are self-evident. Additionally, when choosing a note topic, you should choose one that interests you and that you will feel comfortable discussing because your law review note will undoubtedly be a topic that you are asked about during interviews.

II. Moot Court

Moot court is practice court. Your school will likely have a named moot court organization, or moot court board, run by students, that runs competitions. You should take part in the competitions and try to get on the moot court board as a third-year student. It is another important marker that employers will look for, and generally, just a great opportunity to practice your skills.

The primary importance of moot court is to practice your oral advocacy. Regardless of what type of lawyer you want to be, oral advocacy is a fundamental skill for all lawyers. Whether you are negotiating the terms of a deal, arguing a motion, talking to a client, or presenting your research to your supervising attorney, you must be ready to speak. Indeed, as a junior attorney, while you may not be the one actually making the deal or arguing the motion,[2]

---

2. You never know what tasks you will get as a junior attorney. If you work for a small firm or a public agency, you will almost certainly be thrown into court quickly. And if you work for a large firm, you may be on a leanly staffed matter and the partner may have a conflict and you may have to step up. There may be an emergency motion or an order to show cause that needs an attorney to appear immediately. It could be anything. Point is, be ready. Further, if you do work somewhere that doesn't provide much opportunity for you to get into court as a junior lawyer, you should seek out opportunities to do so, which can be found by doing pro bono cases. Doing these things will distinguish you as a junior lawyer in your firm.

you will be expected—from day one—to present to your client. And as a junior attorney, while you may not present to *the* client, your client is the person you report to: the partner, the senior associate, the head of your department, or the business personnel. Your goal will be to convince your client that your conclusions are correct and accurate so that they can act on your conclusions. That requires oral advocacy. Besides your first-year oral argument in your writing course, moot court may be the only other place to practice your oral advocacy.

At the heart of oral advocacy is trust. Remember, there is a practical purpose to all this—convincing another to act. And in order to convince someone to act, they must trust you, which requires that you provide them with good reasons to do so. Generally, people quickly reach conclusions that they generate on their own. But they do not as easily accept conclusions presented from others. That skepticism makes sense on a fundamental level. We are built to act quickly on information we trust. When that information comes from ourselves, we trust it quickly and act. When it comes from others, we are skeptical. That means people need more reasons from others to accept a conclusion than they would need from themselves.[3] So, as an oral advocate, you must provide good reasons for someone to accept your conclusion. Doing that involves the same process we have discussed over and over again—it is the same framework of argumentation we discussed in Chapter 2—it is the application of the issue to the law and the facts. Once you've put that to paper, you just need to talk about it and convince them you've done your homework.

All this means is that you know the information cold. Know the background facts, the issues, the cases, and how it all fits together. Know what facts you don't know. Know what types of information the cases didn't discuss. Do your homework, study, and then trust yourself. Be ready to present your argument, just like you would on paper, and be prepared to answer questions. Anticipate what questions someone reading your material would have and practice your answer. Be ready to pivot back to the conclusion you presented on your paper. Be ready to concede what you don't know (which, ideally, should be information you can't know—facts you don't have, cases that don't exist). Practice all this out loud. Sound familiar? This is exactly the same principles we discussed in Chapter 4 when providing a framework for your first-year oral argument. And the same preparatory techniques we discussed there apply here.

3. Mercier & Sperber, at 231.

Moot court also allows you to practice your writing since some moot court competitions involve drafting trial memoranda, including pre-trial motions or even pre-trial briefs. You can go even further to distinguish yourself by getting on the moot court board. These school-specific moot court boards typically require you to distinguish yourself in some way; some require you to place in your second-year moot court competition, others by an "argue-on," others by grades, and so on.

CHAPTER SIX

Frameworks for Finishing Strong

You've done it. You've hit the marks. You got good grades, made law review, and you're on moot court. You probably already have a great job ready when you graduate. Congratulations. Enjoy it.

But there is still more work to do. You need to finish strong. You need to set yourself up to succeed. To do so, you need to consider what upper-level courses to take, paper or exam courses, how many, what professor, and the time commitment of each, among others. You will need to consider whether to take a clinic or an externship, or both. You will need to think about balancing all that and your job. And maybe you still have somewhat of a personal life as well. Bottom line is that you need to seriously consider all those factors so that you can set yourself up to maintain that great GPA you worked so hard to get.

I. Choosing Upper-Level Courses

When choosing upper-level courses, your primary consideration is your time. Time is the most valuable commodity you have. As discussed in Chapter 2, managing that time will be a critical skill that you must master. Take on too much work and you will drown; take on too little and you will flounder. As a law student, your first chance to develop this skill when it comes to your every day schedule comes with choosing classes. While taking classes that interests you is important, it is secondary to your time. You must first think about your time so that you can set yourself up to succeed.

When you pick classes, consider the time commitment for each class and compare that to the time commitment for your other classes. The first thing you should do when thinking about time commitment for classes is consider the exam schedule. Now that you've had some experience studying for exams, you know how long each step in the process takes. This means you know that you must start your outline X weeks before the exam and devote X hours each week to your outline in order to be done with your outline X days before the exam so that you can take X number of practice exams and then take the day before the exam off. Consider the time for each of those steps along with the scheduled exam time and how many other classes you are taking. Consider all that against the paper classes you are taking. Remember that paper courses tend to take more time. So don't bulk up on paper courses to avoid exams. If you have two papers due the same day, that may be more difficult than two exams on the same day. Think about whether the paper will be due at the same time an exam is happening. Consider when you will prepare your papers in connection with how many exams you have and their schedule.

After you've considered your time, consider the professor teaching the course. Think about whether that professor has a track record. Can you find previous exams from *that* professor that will help you prepare for *that* test? Consider the professor's reputation for grading. Some teachers grade harder than others. Some professors want more face time in class. Some less.

Consider whether the professor is new or seasoned. New professors can sometimes be tougher than established ones. They are learning just like you, and being their guinea pig is not always the best idea. They may have something to prove or they may have unrealistic expectations of law students because they just came out of years of practicing law. Perhaps the worst part of new professors is that they have no track record with exams. You can't use old exams to prepare, and they have no idea how to write them. They don't know what they are looking for, and they don't know how much to put into an exam. Usually, they expect too much. They cram too much into an exam and make it impossible to finish within the time limit. Experienced professors, however, know how much time it takes to answer their questions. They've made the mistakes. They've asked too much. Made exams too hard. They have refined their exams to a point where they put in just enough information and questions for the time allotted that provides just enough for them to grade. They even follow patterns so you can look at old exams and be fully prepared for their exams. Some have even been known to fully recycle exams.[1]

---

1. *See*, *supra*, Chapter 3 n.9.

That is not to say that all experienced professors are better than new ones. It can certainly go the other way. Indeed, you will hear about the old, cranky professor who has been at the school for decades and never gives an A, no matter what. If you know that, then avoid that professor. Don't think you will be the one student that gets the one A. It's just not worth it. No one looking at your resume will care that you got an A with some locally known hard professor; what they will look at is your final GPA. That's it. So make it count.

You don't need to choose classes based on whether they are on the bar exam. Taking bar exam subjects doesn't matter. You will take a bar exam course for every subject on the exam, so don't feel like you must take evidence or family law or trusts and estates if you don't want to. You will learn all you need to know about every bar exam subject in your bar exam course (which, you *must* take).

In short, set yourself up to succeed by considering your time, the exam schedule, the papers, the type of class, and the professor. Once you've done all that, consider your interests. You should certainly take things that interest you, but that can't be your only consideration. If you can't ace those courses, it won't matter—you will know a lot about your own interests, and no one will care if your grades are no good.

II. Clinics

Taking a clinic is one of the best experiences you will have in law school. You will finally get to apply all the concepts you've learned to the real world. You will get to take on real cases, with real people. And you will get to do so with the guidance (and protection) of your clinic professor. But with all that comes a significant time commitment. More than you think. In a clinic, you will get a taste of practicing law. You will be rewarded with a huge amount of credits (sometimes clinics are up to 8 credits), but it will take a huge amount of time. You will need to take a light course load when taking your clinic course.

Clinic grading is a bit of a black box. It is unlikely you will be graded on a single paper or exam. Instead, you will be graded on several intangible things like your participation, your interaction with clients, interaction with the court, your writing, your preparation, or whatever else moves your professor that day. The one thing you can do is look at the way the professor has historically graded. Check with students who have taken the class before; they will have a good idea of what type of grades the professor gives. Some clinic professors just give everyone Bs, and some all As. But generally, grades do not fall below that. If you are taking a clinic with a professor that gives everyone Bs you may want to rethink taking that class. As mentioned, clinics are generally a large number of credits. So getting a B for 8 credits could be a big hit to your GPA right at the end of law school—so you need to think about that carefully. Again, you don't want to take a clinic for something you love if the professor just hands out Bs to everyone and you are on your way to a 4.0 GPA. You can (and should) do the type of law you want to do, but you won't be able to do that in the real world if you are haunted by a low GPA.

III. Externships

Externships are courses where you work in a legal setting outside law school, generally with a judge. You may have a class that meets once a week, or less, just to check in and share experiences. You may have to keep a journal or write a paper. But this experience is really for you. It will likely be pass/fail or non-graded in some way, so this is a great time to really investigate something that you like and work with someone that can really teach you.

IV. Working While in Law School

Most of us need to work and all of us like money. But, for the time being, you've chosen to go to law school. You've made the decision that the benefits of going to law school outweigh the time, stress, and costs (and the costs are many). One cost is that you need time off during exams. You must take this seriously. There is no juggling at this point. Your exam is the number one priority. Period. Your grades are the first thing employers look at when you exit law school. You want your law school career to translate into a legal career, so treat it seriously.

It takes time to prepare for exams. Your professional work as a lawyer will take a lot of time. Regardless of the complexity of the facts, everything you do as a lawyer is a time-consuming activity. That is why lawyers charge by the hour and not the result. Get used to it. Take it seriously. Do not overload yourself and do not feel guilty about taking the time you need to prepare for your exams.

That is not to say you should not work while in law school. Even if you don't need to, you should seek out work with a local attorney. You will likely get hands-on experience with a real attorney doing real work. You may get to read, or even draft, portions of briefs. Even simply reviewing such material will translate into a better work product in law school.

CHAPTER SEVEN

Frameworks for Beyond Law School

If you've done well in law school, you will undoubtedly have many options. From government work, public interest, clerkships, to law firms, you will have your pick. You are finally ready to reap the benefits of all those years of hard work—which is more work.

To get that work, your great performance in law school will get your foot in the door wherever you want, but you will need to pass some more tests. The first test is the interview process. And the second test, if you are seeking a job at a large law firm, is the summer associate program. After all that (and the bar exam), only then will you finally get to work. And then you will be tested every day in your practice. This chapter provides some tips to get through the interview, the summer associateship, and your first years as a junior associate in a law firm.[1]

I. The Interview

The entire point of all your hard work in law school was to get an interview so you can find a place to practice law. When you apply for legal jobs, not only will you submit your resume and perhaps a writing sample, but you will also submit a transcript of your grades. That is why your priority in law school was to keep your grades high. It is the first thing potential employers will look at. And it is what gets you that first interview.

---

1. Because my experience has been at a large law firm, these tips are geared toward that end—though I imagine they would translate in many aspects to government work or clerking.

Beyond that, getting through the interviews and ultimately getting the job is based on factors you cannot control, including luck. You will never know what baggage your interviewer is coming to the interview with. Or what they are looking for in a candidate. Or the pool of candidates. Or if your personality matches with theirs. Or if you are giving off any unconscious cues that you cannot control. The best you can do is be prepared to discuss anything on your resume (including your past education, jobs, or any type of "soft" parts of your resume, like skills and interests).

You also want to be prepared to demonstrate that you can discuss the law and think analytically. To do that, you might be asked to discuss a writing sample you've provided or something more open, like a paper you have written (maybe for law review or your first-year writing course). The point from the interviewer's perspective is to get you talking about an issue of law and see whether you can think analytically. So be prepared to discuss the writing sample, or an issue you've researched and are familiar with. You do not need to know everything. It is not a test. But you should be able to demonstrate that you can tackle an issue and discuss it.

Interviewers are also looking for someone who has a good work ethic and whom they want to spend a lot of time with. Working at a law firm involves long hours with the same people. So sometimes what the interviewer is really looking for is whether they think you are someone who can fit into the culture of the firm and someone they want to spend long hours with. Of course, whether you pass that test is entirely beyond your control. The best you can do is be prepared and be yourself.

II. The Summer Associate

Many large law firms have summer associate programs. It is generally a six- to eight-week program at the end of your second year of law school. You will get a preview of what it will be like to be a junior associate. You will get all the basic trainings, from technology to firm policy. You will get assignments. And, of course, you will be taken to many lunches, dinners, and other social activities.

For tips on approaching your assignments and the day-to-day in general, review the section below on being a junior associate. The same tips for succeeding as a junior associate apply to being a summer associate. It is not much different from your first year, except you will have much less work as a summer associate than you will as a junior associate. Your assignments will range from research memos, to some document review, to fifty-state reviews of the law, to writing portions of articles, to presentations, to name a few. Mostly, though, you will focus on research and writing. The section below explains how to understand the assignment, conduct the research, and provide a finished product. Review that and the other tips and you should be more than prepared.

As for all the social activities, they may feel like mini interviews, but they are really intended to just be fun for both you and the attorneys in the firm. The best you can do is be yourself. You will almost certainly get the job if you don't do anything terrible. At this point, you have probably heard horror stories about summer associates doing awful things, which range from simply being rude to getting into actual fights. These mostly involve drinking too much. So avoid that. Also avoid any sense of entitlement; that is never received well. If you act normal and get your work done on time, you will almost certainly get the job. Remember, the firm wants to employ you. They chose you as a summer associate. The default, then, is that you will be hired. So do your best to get all your work done and try to enjoy it.

III. The Junior Associate

Once you've made it out of law school and taken the bar exam, you may find yourself starting work at a law firm. Success as a law firm associate is not as easily measured as it is in law school. There are no grades here. No exams. No law review. And no mock competitions to win. At the end of the day, what matters is keeping your job. Whether or not that happens depends on the quality of your work, your relationships, personality, and luck.

Some of that you cannot control. As discussed above, luck is beyond your control. From the big to the small, luck can make or break your career. Whether it is a once in a lifetime pandemic that destroys the economy, your train breaking down before a big court appearance, or waking up to a cold, all of that can affect your success. Dealing with those situations is beyond what any book can teach you.

Your relationships and personality, too, are beyond the scope of this book. It is important, though, to recognize the importance of each. The relationships you have with your coworkers and your boss(es) (all the partners) is affected by your personality, and the better relationships you have, the more likely they are to keep you around.

As to your personality, and as with the other advice, the best I can say about that is to be yourself. Unless you are cocky and arrogant. Then don't be yourself. Be humble. Be a team player. Learn the names of everyone in your office. Remember, "a person's name is to that person the sweetest and most important sound in any language."[2] Also, focus on other people rather than yourself by asking them questions about themselves. In general, people don't want to hear about you; they want to talk about themselves.[3]

Do your best to graciously accept criticism. Don't get defensive. You get nothing from arguing with a partner about why you actually did something right. Just accept the critique and move on. There is likely much for you to learn anyway.

Finally, whatever you do, be kind to everyone, including and most importantly, all the staff. Paralegals and legal secretaries can make or break you. You will need their help, and they will undoubtedly know more than you when you arrive (and likely long after). Not only do you need them, it is just common decency to treat all staff as equals. So, don't be the person who orders people around or acts entitled. And when you need help (and you will need lots of it), ask nicely and appreciate their time as much as your own.

Now for some tips on doing the actual work.

A. Research Assignments

Research is the heart of your work as a junior associate. You will be asked to look at all types of legal questions, all the time. Luckily, this is what law school best prepared you for and a skill you can hone. The same skills you learned in law school apply to your research as an associate (and, I would imagine, forever).

1. Understand the Assignment

Before you do anything, it is key that you understand the assignment. That requires you to fully understand the issue. Some partners are great at asking questions. They know exactly what they are looking for and present the issue directly. Others, not so much. It is your responsibility to make sure you understand what you are being asked. If it is unclear, say so. If you are given an assignment in person, repeat the task in your own words before you leave the room. If an email is ambiguous, respond by repeating the issue in your own words. Tell them what issue you will research. By responding with a statement

2. Dale Carnegie, *How to Win Friends and Influence People*, at 79 (1936). If you need help with your personality, I suggest reading and following the lessons in Dale Carnegie's classic book. They are timeless and worth a read (even if you think your personality is flawless, which, if you do, is probably a good reason to read that book).

3. Carnegie, at 52.

of the issue, you will test your understanding and give the partner an opportunity to correct you.

Once you understand the issue, make sure you know your deadline, the form of the end work product expected (some people call it a deliverable), and the jurisdiction.

First, know your deadline. You may be given an explicit deadline or you may not. If you are not given one, make sure you ask when the finished work is expected. But don't just say, "when do you need this?" There is nothing wrong with that, but that doesn't give you any control over your own schedule. Instead, say something like, "does end of day [date] work?" Think about how long it may take you to research the issue and what other things you have on your plate. Then double that time, at least in the beginning, because it is hard to gauge the time it will take you to accomplish tasks as you start practicing, and it's even harder (sometimes impossible) to account for what may come up in between. If you are given a deadline, make sure it works for you. If it's too quick, ask for more time. But if you do, try to give the partner a sense of what other assignments you have to justify why you need more time. Sometimes, of course, work will need to be done faster than you'd like, but if it is not a true emergency and you think another day may help, ask for it. It is better to ask for more time and produce your best work than to rush and give less than your best. When you do get a deadline or set one, make sure you always meet it. Always. While you can ask for more time if you need it, that should be a last resort. Never just blow past a deadline. If you are going to miss a deadline, you need to communicate that as early as possible and explain why.

Second, the deliverable. For this, you want to find out what form of work product is expected. Ask if they expect your work product in an email, memo, PowerPoint, or an oral report (the last is unlikely and should be avoided—it is better to have it all in writing). You can also ask if they have thoughts on the length of the work product. While they may have no clue how much information is out there or how much paper it would take to answer the question, they may have an expectation or at least know how much they want to read before they get annoyed. If you don't get direction, as a general rule of thumb, less is always more. The final word on length is always that you should use only as much space to answer the question with support. No more. Good writing is concise writing. And, as a lawyer, you are a professional writer. So, get comfortable with writing and take it seriously. Moreover, most partners in a law firm are incredibly busy. They need a quick answer that they can act on. So, don't expect to write law review type articles. Write only what is needed to answer the question and include only as much information as you would need to act on it if you were the partner.

You may also want to ask the partner how long they expect you to spend working on the assignment. But be careful—that is a dangerous question. On the one hand, you do not want to bill more time than expected to research an issue. That can be seen as inefficient and many clients do not want to pay for excess time (you are very expensive). On the other hand, you must take enough time that you are comfortable with researching the issue. And you are learning so it will take more time. It is a balancing act, but it is better to err on the side of taking more time. The partner can always cut your time in the bill to the client. If they are a good partner, they will understand that you are learning as well. But worse than taking too long is getting the answer wrong. If you do get it wrong, you will have to put in more time doing more research anyway. Even worse, you may not be asked to do more work for that partner. And if a partner doesn't want to work with you, you've, in essence, lost a client.

Indeed, think of your partners, or even senior associates, as your clients. For now, they are the ones who give you work and keep you employed. In that sense, they are very much like a client. If they like your work, they will become repeat customers. And when you have to bill 2000 hours a year, you need partners who feed you work. They get the work from the client; you get the work from them. And many law firms have an entrepreneurial internal aspect to them. While, at first, you will be given assignments from some sort of assignment queue or assigning partner, many partners bypass that queue and go straight to associates they like. In that way, there is a sort of free market for associates in law firms. Partners use the associates they like. They fill their time. Take them under their wing. You will usually wind up working for a small group of partners this way. So, treat your partners like clients, do good work, and you will get their business.

Lastly, you need to be clear on what jurisdiction you are searching in. This is not law school—you are not just interested in a basic legal rule regardless of where it came from. You are answering a question that relates to a case in a specific jurisdiction. If it's not clear from the question or materials you are given, always ask what jurisdiction you should research. They will tell you. It should never be a mystery. While sometimes you can stray into other jurisdictions for persuasive authority, you should only do that if your jurisdiction does not answer the question.

Also, if you can, find a senior associate who has worked with your partner before, and ask them if they have any samples or tips for working with or writing for that partner. Many law firm partners have quirks on writing. For example, a partner may prefer oxford commas (right), or they may prefer not to have oxford commas (wrong), but their preference is the right one for your purposes. Certain partners may also prefer underlining cases (wrong) rather than italics (right).[4] Or they may like square bullet points rather than circle bullet points (who knows why). Or they may not like sentences to begin with conjunctions ("and," or "but") because they were taught English long ago (there is no problem with using conjunctions at the start of a sentence). Or maybe they have a strong feeling about one space or two spaces before a sentence (until the legal industry changes, it is two spaces for lawyers). If your partner has quirks, it is likely that another associate knows about it because they have been scolded for not following them. Try to get the benefit of that wisdom early and avoid those small gripes.

2. The Research

This section is not intended to be a substitute for all the learning you did in law school about research. In fact, if you did well enough in law school to get hired as an associate, you are probably a good researcher. Rely on the same skills you learned in law school. Use your favorite research site and look for the cases or statutes that answer the question. Simple as that.

But it's never really simple. Especially in practice. That is why it is on your plate. If the partner knew the answer, they would not ask you. Almost every time you get an assignment, you'll hear something like, "there has to be a case that stands for X," or "there has to be a case where this has happened before," and that it "shouldn't take you very long." That is all wrong. There is not a case where the exact same situation occurred. There is no case that easily answers the question. You will need to piece the answer together from somewhat similar situations.

When you are thinking about research and key words, think about the facts of your case, the claims or relief sought, and the procedural posture of the case. If it's a breach of contract case, the word breach should appear in your search, or rescission if it relates to that relief. If it's a question relating to a securities claim, the word securities should be in your search. If it's a claim about tortious interference, those words should be in your search. Pay close attention to the facts as well. The most persuasive cases will have similar facts to your case. But not all the facts will (or can) be the same. Remember that using analogies does not require that all the facts match up. The more similarities you have, the better the analogy. So try to put a few key facts in your search—maybe something related to the industry, the product, the underlying acts, or

---

4. Underlining is a relic of typewriters. It used to be the only way to provide emphasis, identify headings, or to set off the case name because old typewriters did not have bold or italics. But underlining makes reading the text difficult. Because you have a computer, there is no need to use underlining.

the relationships between the parties. You can also attempt to put in a few words on the legal proposition you are trying to support. Many times a partner will think the law should be some way and ask you to find that rule. The Westlaw and LexisNexis search functions are very advanced. If you put in a few words that resemble the proposition, then they are likely to find the best cases quickly (if they exist).

Finally, keep in mind the procedural posture of the case you are researching—the part of the case you are in. This is something that may be new to you that was not taught in law school. But as a practitioner, it is important to principally rely cases in the same procedural posture as your case. For example, when you are researching for a motion to dismiss, rely on cases that are deciding a motion to dismiss only. If you are researching a question relating to summary judgment, rely on cases deciding summary judgment motions. If you use cases from a different procedural posture, that becomes a weapon for the other side to distinguish those cases from yours.

To summarize, the three important key words to include in any search is the type of case (e.g., contract, personal injury, securities claim), a fact or two going toward the issue you are researching, and the procedural posture (e.g., motion to dismiss, motion for summary judgment).

Once you start finding a few cases, click on the cases those cases cite. Then click on the cases those cases cite. And so on. Go as far down the rabbit hole until you start seeing the same cases being cited over and over, or the cases get too old or too far from the facts.

Regardless of factual similarity, always make sure you are citing binding authority from the highest court in your jurisdiction. Also be on the lookout for cases from your specific judge. You can even run searches looking for cases with your specific judge. If you don't know the judge on the case you are researching, ask.

Focus on cases rather than secondary sources. That is because, in practice, you will rarely, if ever, cite a secondary source in a submission to a court. When you are making arguments to a court, you need primary cites. Sometimes a secondary source can point you in the direction of leading cases if you are stuck, but usually, you will find those cases if you are searching correctly. When you see cases repeatedly referring to the same case, you will know you've hit the right cases. And when you start coming across the same cases in subsequent searches and not finding new ones, you will know your research is done.

If your research concludes that the partner is wrong, or that the law does not allow you to make the argument the partner would like, you must be clear and unequivocal about that. But try not to give just the negative answer. Instead of simply saying that the strategy cannot be done, offer an alternative solution.

If you have been looking through case after case with similar facts and claims and procedural posture, you will undoubtedly come across numerous arguments that other parties have asserted. It will be obvious as you read which arguments may apply to your situation. Point out that you can make an argument you've seen in the case law and support it with the case you found it in.

3. The Research Memo

In your first-year legal writing class you likely wrote a memo. Your professor taught you the format. Writing a memo at a firm is really no different. Many firms have some sort of format for a memo, with a header that has their firm logo and a "to," "from," "date," and "re" (subject) line. It may even provide an outline of the sections. Ask a senior associate for a sample. But the form will be the same no matter what. It is the same form as all good legal analysis—IRAC. The big difference is that you will include a fact section as well. Here is a sample form:

Law Firm Header

To: Partner

From: Associate

Date:

Re: Case Name—Research on [Subject]

I. ISSUE

- Identify the issue. Writing the issue statement can either be as simple as a one-sentence statement starting with whether, or you can use the deep-issue statement discussed in Chapter 4.

II. SHORT ANSWER

- Summarize the answer to the issue. Try to get the issue and short answer on the first page. Remember, partners are busy and need to get the answer quickly. Also, any reader of any material needs to see things quickly or they get bored. The same principles apply to legal writing as other writing.

III. BACKGROUND

- The background section should include all the relevant facts. Do not assume familiarity from your audience, even if the partner gave you all the facts. This section should include all the relevant facts any reader would need to understand the analysis. Your memo may very well be passed on to people who are not as familiar with the facts as the person who assigned the issue. Your email may be forwarded to other people in the firm, or even the client.

IV. ANALYSIS

A. Subheading 1

- The use of headings and subheadings are critically important. They provide roadmaps and break up your writing. Long paragraphs and sections without breaks make it much harder for people to focus. Good headings and subheadings guide your reader. They also provide white space in the document that aids readability.
- For the top-level subheading, use bold font and capitalize each word.[5] Use letters for first level subheadings, A, B, C, etc. If you have another level of subheadings, use italics and regular sentence case with a period at the end. Second level subheadings use numbers, 1, 2, 3, etc.
- For the paragraphs within each section, follow the familiar form of rule, analysis, conclusion.

V. CONCLUSION

- Answer the issue. Use an appropriate indicator phrase, like, "in sum," "in short," "in summary," "in closing," and then answer the issue posed in one or two sentences.

When you send the memo, make sure to include all the backup. Any documents you cite in your background section and any cases or statutes should be sent along with the memo.

5. For fonts in general, you should use serif fonts (the ones that have "feet" on the letters, like Times New Roman) for material that is intended to be read on paper and sans-serif fonts (the ones without feet, like Arial) for material that is intended to be read on a screen.

As a general writing tip for memos, remember that less is always more. Be concise. Strive for a five-page memo, but if you need a bit more, try to keep it under ten pages. It is a rare research issue that needs more than ten pages. You may find that page limitation difficult, but good writing is hard. It takes time and rewriting to say what you want in less space, but when you do, and when you struggle with doing that, you will sharpen your writing. You will cut out the fluff and get to the important facts and law quicker. And your partners will appreciate it. Same with courts. No one wants to read more than they must. There is plenty to read and plenty to do. Your audience's time and attention are limited. Make it easy on your reader and get the information out quickly and easy to understand.

Finally, make sure you schedule your time for researching, outlining, writing, and proofreading. For example, if you have a three-day turnaround on an assignment, plan to take the first day to research, the second to outline and write, and the third to proofread. No matter how much time you have, always schedule time to proofread. This is absolutely necessary—every time. Your memo must be free of typos and grammatical mistakes. Read it out loud; good writing usually sounds good. If you can ask another junior associate to review it, that is great. Regardless of whether you are lucky enough to find a proofreader, you must proof it yourself. Make sure you take some time away from the writing before proofing it yourself. Make sure you print it out on paper. Reading it on paper can help you spot typos. If you have to proofread on a screen, try changing the font, the color of the text, or zoom in or out. Anything that makes the page look different. When you look at the same format of text over and over you are likely to miss typos. By changing its form, it loses the familiarity and helps you spot typos.

Once you've submitted your memo, if it feels appropriate, ask for feedback. Not right away, of course, but a week or so after you submit the assignment. Feedback is important. You need to learn and, while getting feedback can be painful, most partners will do their best to be kind while guiding you in the right direction. If they are not, or if they are not willing to give you feedback, then you are working with the wrong partners anyway.

4. The Email Memo

Often you will be asked to summarize your research in an email rather than a formal memo. Do not treat this as an opportunity to be any less professional and formal than you would be in a standard memo. All the same considerations that apply to a formal memo apply to an email memo. The biggest difference is length; research on email will be shorter and contain less detail.

But it will have the same elements. It will tell the reader the issue. It will tell the reader the rules. It will apply the rules. And it will offer a conclusion. Below is a sample format.

> To: Partner
>
> From: Associate
>
> Subject: [CASE NAME]: Research on [SUBJECT]
>
> ---
>
> Partner,
>
> You asked me to research whether [ISSUE]. In short, the answer is [ANSWER].
>
> A full explanation is below, and the referenced sources are attached. I am available to discuss at your convenience.
>
> Best,
>
> Associate
>
> *****
>
> [Insert a full analysis as you would in a memo. If it makes sense to use headings and subheadings you can do that. If not, follow the same pattern as IRAC, but drop the issue since you stated it above.]

B. Emails

You will email all day, at night, and maybe in your sleep. It will be your primary method of communication. Treat emails as formal correspondence. No typos. No jokes. Do not just fire them off without thinking. If you can, take some time between drafting an email and sending it. Write the email, walk away and do something else before coming back to read it again. Then re-read it again before sending. Do not write anything you would not want a judge (or your mom) to read. Expect every email to be public. They might be. Emails are forever.

If you are ever emailing with an adversary, make sure to always be cordial, and always look like the reasonable person in the conversation. Do not fight with adversaries over email. You get nothing from it. Instead of thinking as if you are writing to the adversary, think as if you are writing to the judge. And you may be. Adversaries are likely to use your words against you at any chance.

And every email you write to an adversary could be Exhibit 1 in a motion. So think about who you are trying to convince; it is not really the other side—it is the person who will read it later, the judge.

When receiving emails from partners internally, the most important thing to remember is to be responsive. That does not mean immediately responding with an answer. In fact, you should not respond immediately with any answer unless you are absolutely certain you know the answer. Same goes for in-person meetings. Before you speak, know you are right or ask to get back to them. If you cannot respond to an email within a short time with the answer (no longer than a half-hour to an hour depending on the email), you should respond with an email acknowledging that you received the email and that you are going to do the assignment. Respond with, "will do," "got it," "understood," or anything short and sweet to let the person know you've received the email and will be doing the work.

Another important aspect of emails is to make sure you keep them organized. Spend a few minutes every day organizing your email into folders and subfolders. Litigation and deals can go for a long time or come back to haunt you years later. The better organized you are, the better prepared you will be to find the appropriate email when you need it.

Another way to keep email organized is to change the subject line of emails when the subject changes. As you already know from normal life, email conversations can take twists and turns. What started as an email chain about scheduling can quickly turn into a request for research or anything else. If it does, change the subject line of the email to reflect the current conversation. For example, you will frequently just get an email with the name of the case or the deal you are working on. That email may start off with a research assignment. When you respond, change the subject line of the email to something like, Case Name: Research on X. You may then get a follow up question on a whole different topic or different case, but the partner probably didn't change the subject line of the email. When you respond, change the subject line to the new case or new topic. It will help you later when searching for emails and keep to break up email chains regarding different subjects.

If you are on emails with clients, make sure you do not email the client without express authorization from the partner. If a client asks you a direct question or you know the answer to a question, take the time to run a draft email by the partner first. Ask them if they'd like to answer and provide a draft email the partner can send. You can never go wrong asking permission, but you can make a significant mistake by sending an email to a client without a partner reviewing it.

Also, when you are on email chains, make sure you read each one even if you are not being asked a direct question. You will likely be kept on many emails where you are not a direct participant. Keep yourself knowledgeable and in the loop regardless. You never know when the information from that email may come up.

Make sure you have an email signature ready that has dial-in information for scheduling calls. Outlook lets you have several email "signatures" that you can append to the bottom of your email. You will have a default one, of course, with your name, your phone number, and email (you need your email on your signature block because when emails get forwarded they can lose your email address in the header). But you should also set up an email signature with your dial-in information. Most firms will have conference call dial-in numbers and you will get your own access line. If you are ever on an email and a call is being set up, you can quickly respond with your dial-in information as a signature. Similarly you will want to get familiar with how to schedule a call for everyone's calendar in Outlook. One easy way to do that is to use the "Respond with Meeting" option, which is under the "Respond" portion of the "Home" tab in Outlook. That will create a meeting scheduling email and you can pop in your dial-in signature. Make sure to schedule a conference room if appropriate. If there are outside visitors, make sure they know how to get to your office, and if your office has security, make sure you arrange for their arrival and give their name to security.

C. Pro Bono

Many firms encourage junior associates, and, indeed, all their lawyers, to do pro bono work. Pro bono work is not only important on its own for what you are doing for others who need access to legal services, but it also provides a great opportunity to get experience early. As a junior associate at most firms, you will not be given the opportunity to conduct depositions, oral arguments, and may not see trial work for a long time, if ever (since cases rarely go to trial). Even as you get more experienced, these opportunities may be few and far between. If you want these opportunities—and you should want them—you can get them through pro bono work.

D. Presentations

You will likely give or help prepare many presentations as a junior associate. You may be giving a presentation at a firm lunch on a current development of the law or a case you are working on, or you may be assisting a partner with a presentation for a conference, or even assisting them with a client pitch.

The basic structure of any presentation is: (1) tell the audience what you are going to tell them; (2) tell them; and, then (3) tell them what you told them. That may be a tired form, but it is the best form for any presentation.

Make sure you use one, simple theme. One of the biggest mistakes is to make presentations too complex. Think of a twitter-friendly headline. For a great example, watch Steve Jobs's presentation of the first iPhone. The theme was "revolutionary." Steve Jobs presented the history of Apple as presenting revolutionary products in the 80s and 90s and then he pivoted to the "revolutionary mobile phone." He used the words "revolutionary" over and over regarding each aspect of the iPhone. It was clear and easy to understand in every slide. It was a simple theme that worked.

Keep your slides simple. Slides are not handouts. Do not use slides with a lot of text on them. Too much text on a slide is a sure-fire sign of a bad presentation. Use the rule of three. The human mind has a limited attention span, and people can only hold three to seven points in their short-term memory anyway.[6] So, keep your slides to no more than three points to be safe.

Further, you should always be showing, rather than telling, in a presentation. To do that, you should be using pictures and words. Using words and pictures together is the best way to ensure both attention and retention. Humans process words and pictures in different physical areas of the brain, so using pictures along with text activates the brain in two different sections, and as a result, people are twice as likely to pay attention and remember your message. By using text and pictures, you are mimicking the way people receive information in their daily lives. People constantly get information in a mix of visual, written, and oral communication. People see, hear, and read a message in their everyday lives. Do the same with your presentation.

Know your audience. Everything must be tailored to your audience. Your tone, message, timing, pictures, language—all must be constructed with your audience in mind.

Talk to your audience; not at them. Your presentation should be like a conversation with friends. You are not reading a speech. You are not just reading off the slide. The slides are aids to your presentation. A presentation is an outline with pictures for you and the audience. The presentation can, and should, jog your memory and guide you for structure, but you should never just read off slides.

---

6. Thagard, at 6, 46.

Tell a story. People learn better through stories. They are attention grabbing. They aid memory retention. They simplify difficult concepts. They even help by-pass defense mechanisms because the story is digested before the listener can put up any defense.

There are three parts to a great story. A likeable hero. A conflict. And the emergence of the hero transformed (the conflict is resolved). If you think that is only for fiction, you are wrong. Every case has a hero—it's your client. Your client encounters a problem. You help them through that roadblock (and in that way, you are another hero). And they emerge transformed when you guide them to the solution.

Work in breaks. A break doesn't have to be a hard stop. You can put in breaks like a short video clip, a poll, a joke, or a handout. These "breaks" help your audience understand what you just said and get them ready to hear another point.

Practice. Get up and run through your presentation. Never do a presentation cold. Hear your own voice speaking out loud. Practice in front of your significant other, family, or friends. They can help you work out the jitters and sharpen your message.

Anticipate questions. All presentations end with the obligatory, "any questions?" No one likes this. But it is always part of a presentation. Try to anticipate questions so you are ready for them.

E. Other Tips

Don't be shy. Tell partners when they are wrong. That is your job. In law school, whatever your professor said about the law was right, even if it was wrong. But it doesn't work that way in practice. Often (very often), partners will think the law must be a certain way. But the more likely scenario is that they *want* the law to be a certain way to make an argument. But the law is the law now. You should do your best to make their arguments work, but when the law is firmly the other way, you have to tell them. Indeed, it is your job to tell them. A good partner will expect that.

Be a great proofreader. One of the jobs you will do as a junior associate is to read other people's work. Just as you cannot leave typos in your own work, you cannot leave typos in theirs. In fact, you might be the last line of defense before something goes out. A good partner will recognize that they too need a proofreader. And that proofreader will be you. They need to trust that you will catch the errors. Early on, being a great proofreader can be just as marketable a skill as being a good researcher.

Get all procedure right. You learned procedure in law school, but you cannot rely on that. You likely learned just federal procedure and you will be practicing in all types of courts now. And they all have different rules. Even when you are in federal court, the court you are in will have its own local rules. And the judge you are in front of will have their own rules on top of that. You need to consult each set of rules, every time you have a procedure question. No one memorizes the rules. You get a general sense of what and where, but every time there is a question, you must check the rule. Moreover, they can often change. Take your time to review them each time you need to file anything.

Be the master of the facts. Another way to stand out in the case is to know the facts cold. A common task for junior associates is document review. It can be, as you've heard, a long, boring slog. But being in the trenches of looking at thousands of documents puts you front and center on the facts. The senior associate and partners will never be as close to the facts as you are. Use that knowledge to stand out. Offer to create timelines and outlines of the facts. These are invaluable.

Know your limits. Do not let anyone put you in a position you are not prepared for. If you need more time or are not comfortable doing something say it.

Safeguard your time. Do not overcommit yourself. If you don't have time, say you can't take on the case. It is better to say no than to say yes and deliver poorly. No one remembers when you say no; everyone remembers when you mess up. Just as in law school, scheduling your time is hard. But it is key to your success. Take on too little work and you will miss your hours. Take on too much and you won't keep up. It is hard to find a balance, especially at a firm, and especially as you start. But you will learn how long tasks take. Always be looking ahead at your week and schedule each day. We all get sidetracked during the day, but if you do your best to keep to that schedule you will be in a better position to get all the work you need done.

Take good notes on phone calls, during meetings, and court conferences. Write down everything you hear even if you don't understand it—and you will likely not understand it. At least if you write as much down as you can, you will have a chance to review it later to understand what was going on. Also, make sure you have a system for taking notes. If you like to write on paper, make sure you have a system for keeping those notes. It may be a good idea to get those notes scanned and stored electronically. You may also take notes electronically, which is preferable. Some people take notes in an email and send it to themselves with an appropriate subject line. Personally, I like to use OneNote, which is a Microsoft Office product that is formatted like a notebook.

You can have virtual notebooks for each case, and then sections for notes that are automatically dated when you open a new page, and a section for research as well. You can also store documents in the pages as well. It is a great program to use as your personal casefile. And it saves automatically. But whatever you use, make sure to always take good notes and that they are organized and accessible.

Anticipate next steps and ask how you can help. Offer to help when a task arises.

Finally, be a team player. Always stand up for your team. Never deflect blame onto someone else. You are a team. You are all working together. There is no competition here among your colleagues. When everyone succeeds, you succeed.

* * *

Transitioning from law school to practicing law is hard. Nothing can quite prepare you for it. But these tips will help you avoid the pitfalls. Focus on doing your work and you will surely succeed. Good luck.

Index